# NOTHING GOOD HAPPENS AFTER MIDNIGHT

---

CONFESSIONS OF A 911 DISPATCHER

PHILLIP TOMASSO

Copyright (C) 2022 Phillip Tomasso

Layout design and Copyright (C) 2022 by Next Chapter

Published 2022 by Next Chapter

Edited by Graham (Fading Street Services)

Cover art by CoverMint

Mass Market Paperback Edition

The conversations in the book all come from the author's recollections, though they are not written to represent word-for-word transcripts. Rather, the author has retold them in a way that evokes the feeling and meaning of what was said and in all instances, the essence of the dialogue is accurate. While all stories in this book are true, some names and identifying details have been changed to protect the privacy of the people involved.

All rights reserved. No part of this book may be reproduced or transmitted in any form or by any means, electronic or mechanical, including photocopying, recording, or by any information storage and retrieval system, without the author's permission.

# ADVANCE PRAISE FOR NOTHING GOOD HAPPENS AFTER MIDNIGHT

"When the desperate call for help the first voice they hear is a dispatcher's, prompting, probing, trying to figure out what the hell's going on. Of course, dispatchers can't see the whole picture and must trust their guides—you, the caller—to show them what's happening. That's how Tomasso tells his own story, abrupt and chaotic, zigging perhaps where you expected him to zag and the result is a book that reads with the energy of the world it's depicting. But amidst the mad delirium is a guy grabbing you by the shirt collar to say hey, I've got a story to tell. A good one. And he's right—this is a damn good story. I recommend you listen." —**Kevin Hazzard, author of American Sirens and A Thousand Naked Strangers**

"Each night, call after call, they handle the traumas, the domestics, the diabetic crashes, the car accidents, the heart attacks, the overdoses, the fires, the drownings, the deaths. Every call for every emergency, sometimes quick fire, and always on repeat. Tomasso's memoir about this under-seen, underappreciated agency is equal parts illuminating, self-effacing, honest, and hilarious." —**James and J.K. Pace, authors of** *Pulse: A Paramedic's Walk Along the Lines of Life and Death*

"As I read the pages of Tomasso's book I was reminded of the hard work done by the dispatchers and call takers in 911 centers across the globe. Accurate and on point, Tomassohas captured the day-to-day life within the comm center and out. Every day our 911 professionals make a difference in the lives of those they serve. Thank you for your service." —**Stephen P. Cusenz, Executive Deputy Director, City of Rochester Emergency Communications Department (retired)**

"This enthralling tale of life in a busy 911 center as told by one of their own kept my attention and left me wanting to hear more. As a retired 911 call-taker, dispatcher, and supervisor myself, I found Tomasso's recollections believable, informative, and captivating. I would loan my copy to friends and relatives so they could learn more about what my life was like when I served in those roles." —**Christopher Martin, Village Justice, 911 Supervisor (retired)**

"NGHAM is a fast-paced, brutally honest depiction of the equally high-speed life of a first responder. Tomasso shares with us his stories of loss and wins and the memories that will forever stick with him, forever change him. His words took me on an emotional rollercoaster, remembering the ups and downs of my own personal calls and the brothers and sisters I responded with." —**Shelby Carr, Retired Firefighter/EMT**

"One word, *groundbreaking*. Not only for the 911 community but also for the friends and families of those wanting a one-on-one glimpse into the world we live in. Truly a one-of-a-kind book. For us, for the friends and family, and for the curious citizen ... this is 911, and you won't regret this read!" —**Morgan Gleisle, 911 Dispatcher**

"A fantastic look into the lives of a 911 dispatcher, Phillip delivers on letting us inside his world of controlled chaos. You laugh at some of the silliness, tear up at some of the sadness, and feel the emotional trauma that dispatchers experience. Confessions of a 911 Dispatcher is a great read for anyone looking to understand what happens on the other side of the line." —**Joshua Taylor, 911 Dispatcher II**

"As a first responder for almost two decades, Tomasso gives a rare insight into the world of dispatchers. Sometimes referred to as 'the first, first responders,' but more often than not they are overlooked in the first responder field. As Tomasso evolves in this autobiography, so does my appreciation for those working the phones and the radio." —**Travis Dobrowsky, Firefighter/EMT**

"Tomasso gives an honest glimpse into the chaotic life of a 911 dispatcher. Many emotions run through you as you read about the good days, bad days, and absolutely tragic days that a dispatcher experiences. This is what it is like to be the very first, first responder.

The voice you hear in some of the worst moments of your life. Truly an amazing read for anyone who wants to gain a better understanding of the real 911." **—Katie Kast, 911 Dispatcher**

"I am not a reader. I read this book in two sittings. There were definitely some chuckles, and I related. I have responded to many calls similar to what Tomasso describes. He hits on points. Some people you can help, and some, unfortunately, do not want help. I truly enjoyed the memoir. It opened my eyes to the daily chaos behind the headset. I am truly thankful for my dispatchers." **—Joel Messore, Rochester Police Department, Police Officer**

"First off, as a career EMS'er this book captured the "other side" very well. OEC is a perspective that is easy to forget and hard to understand. The First Responder battle of the scales; family vs. work vs. sleep vs, sanity was spot on. The effects of absorbing so much trauma and drama although physically disconnected from it is a side not often talked about. Phil did a great job of summing up the feelings and states of calls without having to tell a ton of stories, although I kinda wanted to hear more. I know there are some good ones left untold. May the phone call be clear, short, and to the point. May the radio transmission be even shorter. May you get to punch out before the sun gets too high in the sky." **—Nikki Ladue, Paramedic, Irondequoit Ambulance EMS**

"One man's road to a new job and a new life. The book tells the story of Tomasso's path to 911 dispatching, and the family he finds and becomes a part of no matter how dysfunctional. If you have ever wondered what it takes to work as a 911 dispatcher then learn from the real deal in his wonderful, funny, and oftentimes heartbreaking memoir." —**Trisha Perry, Mindjacked Book Reviews**

"I started as a 911 Fire Dispatcher / Telecommunicator and am now a Rochester Police Officer. I've experienced the emotion, chaos, and struggle Tomasso writes about from both sides of the phone and radio. Exposure to tragedy brings trauma—the caller's trauma becomes your trauma and leaves a lasting impact on your life. Day in and day out, First Responders show up and Do. Their. Job. Many times without thanks and rarely learning the outcome of whatever they dealt with. It's important to remember the sacrifice made each day by everyone in the field. I pray you never have to call in an emergency, but I hope after reading this memoir when you hear *9-1-1 what's the address of your emergency* you take solace knowing strong, brave, hardworking men and women, just like Tomasso, are ready to help you on the worst day of your life. Phil, thank you for your friendship and your service." —**Steve Tucker, Rochester Police Department, Police Officer**

"Nothing Good Happens After Midnight'... Not just a title, but a true sentiment. After nearly 16 years in Public Safety, in different roles and positions, I've worn a few hats. No task has ever been more challenging than that of the Emergency Dispatcher/Telecommunicator. The true heroes, and the first, first responder. This book gives great insight of what it means to tote that thin (very thin) Gold line. The stories told here are just a glimpse into what a 911 Operators and Dispatchers see and deal with. I will never forget where I came from, and where it all started for me. A good read and highly recommended for any and all." —**Michael Lonville; Firefighter/EMT, Deputy Sheriff, 911 Dispatcher**

*This one is for my 911 Family
And, as always,
For my "normal" Family*

*But, I would also like to dedicate this work to
those we lost from our 911 center
during my time with ECD (2009 - Present)*

*Tomasz Kaczówka (1993 - 2012)
Andy Jennings (1972 - 2015)
Marty Kester (1962 - 2016)
Craig Warshawsky (1970 - 2021)
Janet Jordan (1986 - 2022)*

We like to say We are Here First When Seconds Count.
We are the Gold Stripe on the Responder Flag, Between the Blue, the Red, the White, and the Green.
We are often the forgotten *first* FIRST Responders, Overlooked, and too often, the Underappreciated Voice Behind the Radio …
—*Phillip Tomasso III*

# CONTENTS

| | |
|---|---|
| Preface | xiii |

### SAY CHEESE

| | |
|---|---|
| Stay With Me on This! | 3 |
| Some Kind of Disclaimer | 5 |
| Kodak | 8 |
| Ironic | 19 |
| The Test | 21 |

### HOME OF THE GOOD BURGER

| | |
|---|---|
| How is This Going to Work? | 25 |
| First Day | 27 |
| Home of the Good Burger | 40 |
| It's A Funeral | 51 |
| There is Blood Everywhere | 60 |
| More Calls ... | 65 |

### AUTOMATIC FIRE ALARM

| | |
|---|---|
| I Can't Do This | 73 |
| Radio Ear | 81 |
| Who'd You Kill Last Night | 91 |
| You Are Cordially Invited ... to Stay | 98 |
| Yes, We Have No Bananas | 107 |
| Pure Shenanigans | 114 |

### TEN-SEVENTY-EIGHT

| | |
|---|---|
| Let's Dispatch Police Cars | 131 |
| 10-9 | 140 |
| All Out of Police Cars | 146 |
| Agita | 149 |

| | |
|---|---|
| More Unbelievable Calls | 155 |
| I Called 911 Once ... Once | 163 |

A WORKING FIRE

| | |
|---|---|
| New CAD | 169 |
| Still No New Pope | 172 |
| (Candid) Stories from the Fire Side | 180 |
| Some Calls You Just Never Forget | 183 |
| The Language Line | 190 |

MENTAL HEALTH ARREST

| | |
|---|---|
| What is the Worst Call | 197 |
| Do the Right Thing | 204 |
| Libations (Choir Practice) / Relationships | 209 |
| Finding the Balance | 215 |
| Looking Toward Retirement | 220 |
| | |
| Afterward | 222 |
| Special Thanks | 224 |
| Glossary of Terms | 225 |
| Sample Platoon Calendar | 229 |
| Current Monroe County Fire Departments | 230 |
| Current Monroe County Ambulance Corps | 231 |
| Current Monroe County Police Departments | 232 |
| About the Author | 233 |

# PREFACE

The one thing I am certain you will notice is the telling of the story as a whole is disjointed. It is not linear. I start at Point A, hit Point F on the bend, and might curve around to include Point P, but I will—I will, I promise—end up reaching Point B.

Besides, linear is boring. My life, depicted in the pages below, is anything but linear. My lines zig and zag, and cross over one another, as it should be.

This book, initially, is meant for 911 employees and First Responders. We are a different breed. Sometimes we don't understand what it means to fit in with people who don't also do the job. We have our own language. Our own unique sense of humor. General readers may find parts of the memoir offensive, maybe because of the language, or because of the blatant facts put forth. I will not apologize for anything written. You have to understand we take the work we do seriously. Sometimes we laugh now but cry later. We have a dark sense of humor because the calls we deal with day in and day out take a toll. Humor is a way to keep reality at bay, for a while, anyway. It is not that we are uncaring or insensitive. We each struggle in our own way just to deal with things. Laughing is sometimes an easy coping method. I even have the theater symbol tattooed on my left forearm. Only with creepy clowns. Laugh now. Cry Later. It hits home. It means something, and the ink is a constant reminder that I am not always okay.

When another 911 employee and First Responder reads my story I want them to relate. If I fill the pages with fluffy, literary language, they won't buy it. I don't mean they won't buy the book; I mean they won't buy I am for real. However, this could be an important book for the general public, and for the friends and family of 911 employees and First Responders.

This will be a book about the search for balance. The balance between working, family, and life. The balance between taking a call for a car parked on the wrong side of the road, and then taking a call where you have to instruct an eighty-year-old woman as she performs CPR on her husband of fifty years, who she found face down in the kitchen on the floor next to the refrigerator.

I'm not here to complain about management. Anyone, at any company, can do that.

The truth is, as Dispatchers we have outside (and inside) forces working against us. We are always understaffed, overworked, and continually dead tired. Some departments and agencies insist on playing for their own team, instead of working together. We often work with one hand forcibly tied behind our backs, as the resources we have access to (like the internet) are extremely limited or more comparable to Little Tikes tools, instead of Craftsman.

So, do I throw a shot here and there, a dig for the

fun of poking the bear? I do. It wouldn't be genuine if I didn't. Do I blatantly pick on anyone, anything? I do not. It is not necessary. That is not the point of the book.

The point of the book is to find balance in a nonlinear, disjointed life, and in a nonlinear, disjointed career.

Honestly, I am fortunate in my career as a 911 Dispatcher, because I actually love what I do, regardless of the management team (just a playful dig. C'mon now, don't take me too seriously. I surely try not to).

# SAY CHEESE

# STAY WITH ME ON THIS!

THE THING I WORRY ABOUT MOST WHILE WRITING this all down is losing the attention of readers from the get-go. I continually ask myself: *Who am I to think my life is worth writing about? Who out there even cares to read the ghastly, humorous, and, oftentimes, outrageous stories I am about to tell?*

It's conceited at best, and maybe narcissistic at the root, but makes me wonder if all memoirs and autobiographies fall between the two. I don't really read them, so I wouldn't actually know.

What I do know is I wasn't a president, a millionaire, an actor, a singer, or a songwriter. I am not anyone with any political power or scientific insight. I never invented anything, didn't win awards, I was not a heroic soldier, did not fight in any wars, and I sure as hell was not an athlete.

So who am I? Why write this book?

My insecurities are sincere and genuine, and yet here I am. I have been jotting down notes for this book for the better part of twelve years. And now I am committed to the writing of my story, and daily, find myself plugging away at the keyboard, categorizing life as a dispatcher into essay-like chapters. Formatting and reformatting ideas inside my brain have been like working tiles on a sliding puzzle. There is a big picture, and I'll get there. Eventually.

Regardless, I sit at the computer for hour after hour getting my career at 911 into order. And yet the question begs, it nags at me, asking—why write this book?

The reason is simpler than I thought. For the answer, you'll have to read along, and by the end, let's see if we come to the same conclusion.

Additionally, I plan on writing this entire book as if you and I were just sitting around in a bar, swapping stories over beers. Except it's all about me, and I can't hear a word you are saying.

I guess what I am asking is if you'll just stay with me on this. I am going to do my damnedest to deliver a fresh, raw, and honest look into my life and into the life of a 911 Dispatcher.

Not all dispatchers. Not even some dispatchers.

Just the revelations of one dispatcher.

This dispatcher.

Me.

## SOME KIND OF DISCLAIMER

Perhaps some kind of disclaimer is needed. I want to put one here, in spite of, or despite, the cookie-cutter disclaimer found at the start of most books. The plan is, to tell the truth about everything. The problem is, the truth told will be from my viewpoint. The way I saw my life as it unfolded. Other real people will be in this book. Some, I will use their real names because I have been given permission by certain people to do so. Many, I will have changed their names. Could be a lot of reasons why I've changed a name. The top reason? There is a good chance I just can't remember their name well enough to ask for permission.

I am notorious with names. *Hey You. Buddy. Peanut. Partner.* Those are some of my closest friends. (Not really. Do you get the idea, though?) Other reasons I've changed a person's name? They didn't want to be mentioned. Maybe they felt as if appearing in this particular book could put their job as a telecommunicator/dispatcher/supervisor with the City of Rochester at risk.

They needn't worry, I don't *think?*

Bullying and targeting are from the bowels of the Employment Dark Ages and, most certainly, are not anything that happens in today's workforce society [salt with sarcasm, liberally]. Regardless, wishes to remain unnamed will be honored.

The last thing I want is wrong impressions. This book isn't meant as an exposé by any stretch of the imagination. The focus of the book will be on the life of a Dispatcher and my life outside of dispatching. Will some feathers get ruffled, I assume so. Not with malicious intent. I am most hopeful family members and friends of 911 employees, and first responders, read this work. It may help them see why we work most weekends, miss holidays, and why some nights (or mornings, or afternoons) when we get home from work all we want is a beer and the television. Or a nap. Or to simply take a walk around the block. Or cut the lawn with headphones on. Why would we *rather* spend time alone decompressing, instead of talking about our day?

I still have a few years before retirement, and the last thing I want is to accidentally place my own job in jeopardy. With that said, I am still going to tell the truth, the whole truth, and nothing but *my* truth.

If you are looking for crazy, wild, funny, terrifying, and haunting 911 calls, you'll get them. They're in here.

You will also get my take on those calls. Insight into how they have changed and reshaped who I am.

We are going to look at life on the floor—the operations floor—of a 911 center that fields just over 1.2 million calls per year, as well as life outside of work.

Okay.

With the disclaimer hammered home, I think the

best thing I can do now is just dive right in. Unfortunately, like most stories, this one doesn't begin with my working at the Emergency Communications Department for the City of Rochester. We'll get there, but not without starting where all great stories start at the beginning.

*No. No. No.*

I am not going to start with the cliche of having been born in Rochester, New York on June 3, 1970, at St. Mary's Hospital. No need for mentioning the 3rd had been a Wednesday, and twenty-seven years before St. Mary's, a Catholic hospital riddled with nuns and brothers and priests as staff, reorganized into primarily a Brain Injury Rehabilitation Unit in a partnership with Unity Health Systems. Facts like that bore me to write, and I imagine bore you to read. While completely true and accurate, they are irrelevant. Don't you think?

# KODAK

It makes far more sense to jump ahead another twenty-one years from the glorious day of my birth, to when I first started working at the Eastman Kodak Company. Let's look more closely at November 1991.

Damn. I didn't want to do this. It's not a loss of focus. Just a readjustment. Let me back this up a fraction more. A quick sidebar, something of a necessary footnote, if you will.

After my freshman year at SUNY Brockport, I failed out. This occurred in late spring 1989. The goal had been to master the Criminal Justice program, earn my bachelor's degree, and land a job as a police officer.

Early on in the first semester, I learned that because of my poor eyesight, I'd never pass a police physical. I made terrible choices after the news and gave up. I concentrated on partying instead of studying. I didn't exactly fail out. They placed me on academic probation and after the completion of freshman year, I just never returned.

I bounced from job to job for a while, until one

day I got a call from someone from Kodak Human Resources.

I remember when the Eastman Kodak Company thrived as its own city within the city of Rochester. There were 145,000 employees worldwide (at its peak).

Hiring me happened just before the digital era destroyed George Eastman's empire, having been informed I would work in maintenance mopping floors, emptying garbage cans, and scrubbing toilets. Armed with only a high school education I accepted the position. Without a crystal ball, and no way of knowing the damage digital technology would inflict, I figured, *hey, at least I got a foot in Kodak's door*.

Turns out, when I arrived for orientation at Kodak, they had a different job in mind for me. I would work as a Film Tester for Black & White, in a hub at Kodak Park, in Building 28. The hub, known as Central Test, sat centered around the rooms where giant rolls of emulsion were coated in layers. Samples cut from rolls during the start, middle, and end of the coating process were sent in light-tight canisters through snaking air tube systems to us for a battery of testing for any imperfections on each coated roll.

In my new position that didn't involve cleaning toilets, I read entire novels on nearly every shift I worked. We worked twelve-hour shifts. Two day shifts, two night shifts, and three and a half days off. Wasn't a bad deal if you overlooked how the schedule wreaked havoc on my insides, destroyed good eating habits, and made it near impossible to maintain any kind of normal sleeping pattern.

During the nineteen years I worked for Kodak, I knew luck stayed on my side. I got to do some moving about within the company. I next ventured into Building 2 where I trained in cutting similar film samples into 35mm strips and running a different variety of tests for quality control and consistency.

Eventually, I took a job in an assembly factory-style area, run at the Elmgrove Plant in the heart of the Gates suburb.

I was married with three kids, at this point. The three kids I still have. The wife, not so much.

The posted Assembly Position listed daytime hours. Monday through Friday. Six in the morning until 2:30 P.M. The idea I could work a more normal schedule made my (then) wife very happy. I admit during the interview for this position I may have lied some. The department needed a handy employee. Like really handy. With tools, and measuring. And tools. Did I already mention that?

The way I saw it? Just the weekend before I put together a lawn mower, one of those you take out of a box, you secure the wheels, and affix the handle to the base. Feeling quite handy after successfully puzzling together a lawnmower, I didn't feel as if I stretched the truth much during the interview.

I had stretched the truth, of course. Just, at the time, it didn't feel that way.

Oh, how wrong I had been. And it didn't take management long to realize I was in over my head. Way over my head. Like, I knew I was drowning, and I couldn't see a life preserver anywhere.

Until, that is, my direct supervisor approached me one day and asked if I knew how to work with computers.

I told him I could handle myself when it came to computers. (This happened in the early 90s, people).

He should have spotted the lie as soon as I spoke it. The way I saw it, I had to. I didn't want to get fired. Oh, the web we weave, right?

They moved me off the assembly floor and into an office cubicle where I wrote assembly manuals. I worked with the assemblers (those who were doing the job I had no skill to handle) photographing step-by-step as they put together the graphic art equipment I could not, myself, assemble. I documented every screw, bolt, twist, and turn. Back in the office cubicle, I married the digital photographs and assembly instructions I'd written together and, using Photoshop and Word, created Key Points which were printed, fit into binders, placed on the assembly floor, and maintained by yours truly.

Thankfully, as it turned out, in this job I performed exceedingly well, and my talent for using a computer and digital cameras did not go unnoticed. Engineers from several different departments "borrowed me" and my services for Key Point manuals on new assembly construction.

In the meantime, Kodak as a whole, hemorrhaged. Digital photography caught on. People stopped buying film. Professional photographers saved tons of money purchasing data cards. Kodak's edge on the market slipped. They hung, barely, onto the face of a cliff with no real hope of scaling their way back to the top.

Company layoffs happened twice a year and, little by little, thousands of people lost jobs during each hellish go-around.

Preparing for some kind of a future, I took night school classes and earned an associate's degree as a paralegal. Part of me figured if I couldn't become a police officer maybe I could do something "law" related.

Just as I graduated, I found an opening within Kodak's legal department. I interviewed with corporate lawyers convincing them I would be a valuable asset to their team. I saw no need for stretching the truth this time, as I'd maintained a 3.9 GPA in school, and my genuine passion for the law became apparent.

I spent my last ten years with Kodak working as an Employment Law Paralegal. I investigated claims of discrimination alleged by employees that were filed with the Equal Employment Opportunity Commission (EEOC), and the New York State Division of Human Rights (NYSDHR). I interviewed human resources personnel, department managers, supervisors, and any employees with the knowledge, or who were witnesses to, the alleged complaint(s)s. Then I prepared a corporate response, citing case law with conviction, ensuring an affirmative defense at every possible turn.

I will never forget one case where a person alleged they had been discriminated against, based on the this-or-that protected right. The specifics don't matter. During depositions, I sat beside an outside law firm attorney representing Kodak. She excelled in her firm and knew the road to becoming a partner lay, perhaps, around the next bend. I worked with her often and admired her skill. Just before the deposition started, I whispered: "During discovery, the defendant submitted their cell phone call log."

"I know," the lawyer said.

"Well," I reminded her, "we subpoenaed the cell company for the same records, and I noticed this..."

I pointed to the copy received from the defendant, and then over at the copy, we had received directly from the cell service provider. A clear discrepancy between the two. One of the documents had been doctored. The attorney's eyes twinkled. I think if it had been appropriate to kiss me, she would have. Not in a sexual way, but definitely in a "Man, I Love You Right Now" way. Which I would have been okay with because I knew such a kiss was deserved!

The best part about now? Watching the painful deposition unfold. I sat patiently by the side of the attorney the entire time. She asked key questions, where the defendant blatantly lied here and there. He clearly thought his sworn testimony fell under consistency, while we knew it only came down to him covering his tracks. What he didn't realize? Each of his answers highlighted the deplorable and dishonest actions he'd taken.

My excitement percolated inside my chest. The tension grew and grew. I enjoyed every second of the deposition. So many times I wanted to wink at the stenographer as if silently communicating to her: "Watch this. Here it comes."

The defendant, sitting across from us with his attorney, had no clue. They were this close to getting blindsided. Forget deer in the headlights. Imagine yourself washing your hair and body in the shower, never realizing the danger right on the other side of that thin clear shower sheer. And then, (queue eerie music) *BAM!* Norman Bates yanks open the shower curtain and...

You know in legal thrillers, or dramas, they always mention the smoking gun?

Altered documents submitted during the discovery period of a legal matter are what they're referring to, it is what they are always searching for. I had found that smoking gun. If I could slip my finger inside the trigger guard, spin the smoking gun round and round and then push up the front of my cowboy hat with the barrel, and grin, and wink, I sure as shit would have.

When the two sets of different documents were placed on the table between the parties, I almost started giggling. That would have been completely unprofessional. Still, I believe I might have smirked.

The deposition ended a few minutes later after the attorney asked one last, simple question: "Can you explain the discrepancies between the document you submitted during discovery and the copy we received with our subpoena to the phone company?"

*Got em! Cut. Print. It's a wrap!*

My job as an employment law paralegal also had me arguing on behalf of the employer at unemployment insurance hearings. At the hearings, held in front of an Administrative Law Judge (ALJ), I loved getting pitted against actual defense attorneys. The attorneys represented former employees who, terminated for cause, applied for unemployment insurance benefits, and were denied. I never went into a hearing unprepared. I would have copies of all documentation in triplicate, the policy violated, signatures on training received, and witness statements. One for the ALJ, the claimant's attorney/former employee, and a copy for myself. I brought supervisors, human resources, and sometimes other employees to the hearings so they could testify on the company's behalf.

Arguing the company position at these hearings always made me feel a little like Matlock or Perry Ma-son. I would use catchphrases like, "Isn't it true..." and "On the morning of..."

Look, I know what you're thinking. How can I feel proud about preventing someone from receiving unemployment insurance?

I did feel proud.

I won approximately 98% of every hearing I participated in. Why? It had nothing to do with any magic performed at the hearings, although some thought I liken to a David Copperfield. No? Penn and Teller? Still no? Houdini? Blaine? When it came to practicing unemployment law, mostly it stemmed from this simple truth: an employee had to have done something habitually wrong, or so unforgivably wrong, termination became the only option. The last resort. Not smoke and mirrors on my part. Nothing up my sleeves. The company kept great documentation. Made my job easier. Oh, and for the 2% of the hearings I lost, I won most of those on appeal.

Lastly, I participated on legal teams when the company fought large lawsuits and class action claims in state and federal courtrooms. The class action suits became nightmares. Giant rooms, like warehouses, filled with boxes of printed emails, reports, or both. Every individual page required a Bates number, not including anything privileged, or part of the attorney's work product. Then grouping, placing into binders, and managing (as well as owning) the entire process. Not nearly as much fun as hearings in front of an ALJ or handling the discrimination complaint cases with the EEOC and NYSDHR. However, I did what needed doing and with a smile, generally.

My office sat on the fourteenth floor of the Kodak Offices, downtown Rochester. If you see the tall

Kodak building in most online photos, the tower with the word Kodak in red lights on the top—was where I worked. I shared a secretary with one of the attorneys. Inside my office sat a coffee table, couch, two chairs for visitors, my desks, filing cabinets, a computer, a telephone, and also a door. I'd graduated from the Elmgrove cubicle. In the summer, I watched the Rochester Red Wings play noon baseball games from my window while I ate lunch. Sometimes the Blue Angels, when in town, made the building shake as they slung around the tower on trips to and from the local airport.

My days were never dull, and I knew I had finally found my true calling. Several attorneys I worked with encouraged me to consider continuing my education and getting a law degree.

Something to think about, and think about it I did.

At this point in time, married with three kids, just like Kodak, my marriage also suffered from some severe hemorrhaging. Until, eventually, it bled out.

Around Easter 2008, my wife of just under fifteen years no longer wanted to remain married. There are plenty of He Said, She Said reasons. I know I didn't perform as the perfect husband, but right now isn't the time for that tale. We will explore more of that later in the book. It doesn't fit in at this point. Not here. Not at the beginning of it all. What you need to know is we separated, forcing me to move out. That, however, might actually be where it all really started. My transformation. Not might. *Is*. It *is* where everything in my world crumbled and changed.

Don't fret. This isn't a *woe-is-me* memoir. I mean, it kind of is. No one's life is a bed of roses. My past most definitely shaped my present (or at the time: my future). There stood a rose or two. Carnations, mostly. A ton of thorns. Let's get that straight right now. There have always been plenty of thorns.

The point is that separation did play a role in changing me from the person I was into the person I became. Whether that is good, bad, or indifferent I can't say. I suppose I became a mishmash of the three. A smushed-up interpretation resembling something Vincent van Gogh might have painted if he were gobbling up edibles and swigging Red Stag from the mouth of a bottle. (His rendition of me would *not* have been considered a masterpiece, even by the blindest of critics. You would never have seen it featured in a gallery or suspended from a nail on the wall, above a urinal in a bar's Men's Room. More than likely the famed artist would have, embarrassingly, just slid the canvas into a sock drawer to be eventually, and hopefully, forever forgotten).

To further muddy waters, my *True Calling*, as it were, got severed (and the idea of going to law school) as film-less photography continued cutting the legs out from under the Rochester-based corporate giant. They crashed from around 145,000 employees down to under 20,000 worldwide. At the end of my tenth year as a paralegal, the corporate legal department felt the impact of Global Downsizing.

At the end of 2008, just before Christmas, I found myself ... tapped.

That's what they called it.

Getting Tapped. When I thought of someone getting tapped, I always pictured some guy working. Earbuds in. Music, making the workload lighter, mentally. Then, from behind, some big boss walks over. He's wearing a starched white dress shirt, sleeves rolled up mid-forearm. He stops just behind the production worker, leans forward, and taps the hardworking man on the shoulder. The man turns around. Boss hands him his proverbial pink slip and offers up useless condolence: "Sorry. We're going to have to let you go."

It's not how it went down. The process outlined contained far more structure. A little more formal. Same punch-in-the-stomach results, though. The same nuts and bolts of the execution.

My generous severance package consisted, basically, of nearly a year's pay, and six months' worth of health benefits. Naturally, I had made a ton of connections. Kodak's legal department worked with a number of employment-based law firms. I knew the city's best and brightest partners, attorneys, firms, and paralegals ... and they knew me.

I interviewed with multiple firms over the next several weeks. While positions were often offered, the pay was horrendous. The pay difference between working as a corporate paralegal compared to a law firm paralegal are astronomical. Accepting a job would have crippled me financially despite my experience and proven track record as a paralegal.

I spent the year applying for any and every job I came across, within reason.

# IRONIC

The severance package Kodak offered the unfortunate tapped thousands didn't last forever. The actual allotment dished out came down to two weeks' pay for each year of service.

I had nineteen years with Kodak, which translated into, roughly, thirty-eight weeks' pay. Not quite a year's salary for doing nothing but staying home, drinking beers, and feverishly hunting around online for a new career.

As time ticked by, I ventured through the doors of a temporary job placement agency. Filled out a ream of paperwork and was rewarded the next day. The agency found me a temporary position. Trick-shifts. Twelve-hour blocks. Guess where? Go on. Guess. Yeah, at Kodak.

I could almost cry. Back at Kodak Park, working in the dark rooms?

Do you know how movie film has holes running along either side of a giant roll? Sprocket holes? That's what they are called. I loaded a roll of film onto a reel-to-reel with no sprocket holes, spliced one end onto a lead, and ran a machine that punched the sprocket holes into the film, rewinding the film on the opposite end of the machine. Mindless work performed in the dark, and a bit backbreaking. Film, in those trademark silver canisters, is not light. Perforating film for an entire shift became immediately monotonous as all get out! One roll after another, filling pallets with stacks and stacks and stacks.

Sometimes a man does what he has to do because it needs to be done. I had child support payments to make. With three kids on the other end, it took a chunk out of an already meager paycheck. Not complaining at all. They are my kids, and I would always do whatever it took to care for them. Including twelve-hour shifts perforating sprocket holes into movie film.

Thankfully, I did not need the position for more than a few months. You see...

# THE TEST

Earlier that summer of '09, aside from sending my applications out everywhere, I did take a Civil Service exam for a position as a 911 Dispatcher with the City of Rochester. Although I had submitted applications for jobs all over the county, this job caught my eye. With always wanting to be a police officer, and then working as a paralegal, the idea of becoming a dispatcher seemed to align, somewhat, with childhood dreams (eyesight be damned).

The Emergency Communications Department (ECD), is the 911 hub for all of Monroe County. In a broad sense, all 911 calls made went to ECD. For the most part, all of the police departments, fire departments, and ambulance companies were dispatched out of the same office.

I walked out of the exam pulling hair from my head, figuring I'd blown it.

Turns out, I scored a 94%. What d'ya know? At thirty-nine years old, my life would begin anew. As a 911 Dispatcher. But you kind of knew that, didn't you? Otherwise, this would be one heck of a short memoir about a dispatcher.

# HOME OF THE GOOD BURGER

TELECOMMUNICATOR

# HOW IS THIS GOING TO WORK?

I HAD NEVER BEEN HAPPIER TO TELL A PLACE OF employment, "I quit." A little bitterness may have gotten the better of me, anyway. After getting downsized from Kodak after nineteen years of faithful service, finding my first job through a temporary agency, back at Kodak, could do that, create some bitterness.

The hiring process for ECD proved something of a red tape nightmare.

The extensive background check conducted by deputies with the sheriff's office lasted weeks. Maybe longer. They called references, and former employers and visited with family and friends. I also needed all of my school transcripts and complete employment history. They wanted banking information, and the promise I would give them my next born child (the joke was on them. I had a vasectomy. There would be no more children produced from these loins, that I will admit to). I also had to undergo an extensive psychological one-on-one interview.

Next came the interview with ECD management. I showed up around fifteen minutes early, and let the lady at the front desk, seated behind bulletproof glass, know. Told her I arrived a bit early and was more than happy to sit and wait. A large man came out from the back a little while later. We shook hands. He verified I was who I purported to be, after looking over my driver's license, and then said, "It is very nice to meet you, Phillip, but you're a little early."

"Way I was raised," I answered. "It's okay, though. I don't mind waiting."

He smiled. "No, I mean like seven days early. Your interview is next Tuesday. Not this Tuesday."

I checked the letter I held in my hand. The interview date—still a week out. Slightly embarrassed, I replied, "I just wanted to express my eagerness for this position."

We shared an awkward goodbye and I left, laughing the entire ride home. I had to laugh; crying would have been completely deflating. Either I'd blown it, or it did actually show genuine intent for potentially gainful employment.

(Obviously, I think we both have some idea of how things turned out. Don't worry. I won't keep doing this).

# FIRST DAY

The city hired me for a Dispatcher position. There are two entry-level positions. The first is as a Telecommunicator (TCC). These are the operators who answer emergency calls, conduct the initial interviews over the phone, and determine the priority level for the incident. Then there are Police Dispatchers, who send police officers, deputies, and state troopers to calls, and Fire Dispatchers, who send fire trucks and ambulances to events. I know that sounds like three entry positions. It isn't.

When hired, you are either a TCC or a dispatcher.

Which side of the room you work as a dispatcher depends on how things fall out during class. When initially hired, I wanted the job of a police dispatcher. Makes sense. I tried criminal justice at SUNY Brockport. I worked for ten years as a paralegal. Why wouldn't I, at the very least, want to dispatch police cars?

Being a dispatcher didn't mean you didn't take emergency phone calls.

You did. Just not as often. It goes in a kind of rotation. If there are six fire dispatcher spots, and seven fire dispatchers working, the person with the oldest phone date went to phones for that shift. Generally, and I suppose on average, dispatchers take 911 calls once a week. Sometimes more. Sometimes less. Depends on staffing.

Class Training plays out like this:

The first month is classroom setting. New Hires learn rules and policies. Some written. Many just assumed and passed down like legends. Urban legends. Next, you learn the Computer Aided Dispatching software, or CAD as it is commonly referred to in the field. This is where TCCs type the information fed to them by the caller.

It is important to note a TCC position has three computer monitors, two keyboards, and two mice, while the dispatch position consists of five monitors, one keyboard, and two mice.

Then the new hires hit the floor. The Training Office pairs the trainees with seasoned veteran TCCs. The trainees spend the second month of employment taking actual 911 calls with a trainer. Both have headsets plugged in, but the trainee will say what their trainer tells them to say, and type what they are instructed to type.

TCCs continue their training with a trainer until they are certified—considered good enough at what they do to work on their own, without a trainer. It didn't mean they wouldn't have questions. We all still have questions. It just meant they were capable. This particular process usually takes an additional two- to three months before certification.

Next, for the dispatcher new hires, it is back to class for the third month of employment, where, you guessed it, one learns how to dispatch. Whether Police or Fire and EMS it depends. Along with learning the mechanics of dispatching using CAD, there are additional binders filled with more rules and countless new policies. Plus, you have to learn terminology (which for many is as foreign as learning a second language), the ins and outs and procedures for the different departments, and numbers. Every police car, fire truck, and ambulance has a number sequence. It is how they are identified. You see these numbers painted onto their vehicles. They are not random. The number sequence indicates a department, a district, a specific piece of equipment, and so on.

After that, you spend up to four more months on different rotations, with different trainers, until you are certified as a dispatcher and prove you can work independently dispatching and taking 911 calls.

A quick breakdown of shifts. We call them platoons. First Platoon is midnight to 8 AM or 0800 hours. Military time. Initially tough to figure out, but it makes things less confusing. There is no question if something happened in the AM or the PM when using military time. Second Platooners worked from 0800 to 1600 (8 AM to 4 PM), and lastly, Third Platoon runs from 1600 to 2400, or 0000 (4 PM to Midnight). Two paid fifteen-minute breaks, and one paid lunch. Not too shabby, eh? Also, it is a four-day work week. Two days off. So the work week is different by one day each week. Works out so an employee gets a full weekend on an actual weekend once every six weeks. (And don't forget about working nights, and holidays, as well. I have spent—to date—ten of the last thirteen Thanksgivings working. The same goes for Christmas, Easter, the Fourth of July, and Halloween).

Anyway, on my first day, I arrived at work early. Not a week early. I learned that lesson when interviewing. Nervous, I sat alone in the breakroom. There were some full-size fridges for lunches, an oven, dishwasher, microwaves, and a variety of extremely overpriced snacks and chilled drinks in vending machines. The breakroom bore giant windows that looked out into the atrium. There were green shrubs, high ceilings with skylights, and eventually, an installed pond with koi fish.

A tall man, dressed in all black, including a black leather jacket, entered the breakroom. Mostly bald, with a gray biker-style mustache, he looked like a man you didn't want to mess around with. His eyes scanned everyone in the breakroom and stopped when they landed on me. I admit I felt as if he were holding back a sneer.

Then he spoke. His unexpected, high(er)-pitched voice caught me off guard. "Do you drive a red Chevy?"

I did, so I said, "I do."

"It rolled into the middle of the parking lot. It's blocked people from leaving and is keeping other people from pulling in."

I drove a five-speed. I must have forgotten to set the parking brake.

Sucking in a deep breath, I didn't even bother exhaling as I bolted out of the breakroom and out of the building. I know my face turned red. I didn't need a mirror to see it, and I surely didn't want anyone pointing it out. Sitting in the middle of the parking lot, quite literally blocking just about everyone, sat my car.

When I climbed into the car, started the engine, and put the thing into reverse, a part of me considered shifting into first, pulling out of the parking lot, and going home. I could easily have written off the day as a loss.

I didn't. I couldn't. I needed this job. More than that, I wanted this job. The pay was very good. There is a state pension. Free health care. A 457 (or Deferred Comp). There was no turning around and going home. I had to stick this out. I had to see the day through.

I reparked the car. I set the parking brake. I double and triple-checked the set brake before exiting the driver's side. With my head hung a little low hiding shame and unflinching embarrassment, even I noticed the missing pep in my step. I shuffled back into the building, the best I could. I walked past the breakroom, eyes on the floor, and towards the backroom where they intended to hold TCC class.

While I sat and waited for the remaining new hires, I, sadly, remembered two very similarly awkward first days from my past...

---

Before my first day of high school as a freshman, the doctor found a growth of skin over a small bald spot on my scalp. I needed the growth surgically removed. The procedure required a patch of hair shaved away from the area and what felt like twenty Novocaine shots into my skull. Although the procedure finished quickly, and pretty uneventfully, it ended with a mummy wrap of gauze bandage around my entire head. With but a single piece of gauze tape, the nurse covered my whole cap (over and behind the ears) in white surgical mesh, and did so with a professional skill I knew, instinctively, my mother would never in a million years, be able to duplicate. Not even with an ounce of the nurse's finesse.

And the next day? My first day of high school.

I wish my assessment of my mother's lack of ability hadn't been so dead-to-nuts.

My first two high school years were spent at a Catholic high school. From kindergarten through eighth grade, I attended St. Theodore's; A Catholic elementary school. When it came time to look at high schools, the idea of going to anything *but* a Catholic high school terrified me. The hard thing about parochial schools is the tuition. Very expensive. With four enrolled kids, my parents despairingly found already tight financial resources stretched paper thin. In order for me to attend a Catholic high school, I needed to pitch in. At fourteen, I started a job as a busboy at the Diplomat Party House. I believe I earned $2.35 an hour. The summer of '84 flew by because I worked between thirty- and sixty-hour weeks. New York State Labor Laws meant nothing to the co-owners of the party house. And they treated their underage, overworked minions like shit. Regardless, I needed a job and money. The Diplomat filled the bill.

Needless to say, on my first day of high school—a scrawny, hundred-pound freshman—I became a skinny ball of jumbled nerves. Catholic high school, or not. I remember clearly wearing rust-colored corduroy slacks, an off-white dress shirt, and a briney brown knit necktie. To top it off, quite literally, an overabundant amount of medical gauze, with snatches and snippets of medical tape, wrapped my head like something more closely resembling used toilet paper with scotch tape, instead of a slightly more dignified ambling mummy. I stood at my locker knowing tufts of my deer brown hair jutted out between layers. What could be done about it? Nothing. Not a single thing.

Worse, my elementary school didn't have lockers. We kept our belongings in coat rooms, or inside lid-lifting desks. Perplexed, anxious, and feeling absolutely like an alien on a foreign planet, I spun the dial on my Master padlock repeatedly without ever getting the sequence quite right. Three turns to the left. Two turns to the right. Stop on the third number. Nothing. Three turns to the right, two to the left, last number. Nothing.

I could have screamed!

Let's complicate matters more, shall we? A young, very attractive girl moved up to open the locker directly next to mine. I saw her peripherally, only. I knew not to slow-turn my head.

God, I knew I already looked like a monster from a B-horror film. The slow head turn would have sealed the perception!

Hands shaking, I went through the process again, and again. I became painstakingly aware of how I must have looked. I am sure I resembled a crazy patient who escaped from a secure hospital wing—shy of an extra longsleeve jacket that buckled in back—with my hair, my inability to open a combination lock, and now my stiff neck because I didn't want to look at her, even though I wanted to turn and look at her.

When she asked if she could help, I had no choice, and so I silently stepped back and gave her the reins. With a friendly smile, she opened the locker, (she immediately became David Copperfield in my book. Look him up if you have no idea who I am talking about), but then also showed me with the Master lock in her hand, how she had performed a feat of magic before my eyes so that I could better understand no trick existed. I was just dumb. Perhaps, unbeknownst to her, she'd proven it.

We introduced ourselves and became friends, thankfully. I still wonder, to this day, if she placed me somewhere on the spectrum (that didn't really exist in 1984), wordlessly explaining why she had been so nice to such a nerd.

Fast forward two years. I am exhausted from putting in forty-hour work weeks while going to school. The restaurant business is brutal and demanding, and I worked every weekend, all weekend long. I missed high school parties, football games, and socializing with anyone outside of the friends I'd made at the party house. Not to mention, I received mostly Cs and Ds in my classes. Who had time for homework, or to study for tests, and exams? I most certainly did not.

My desire for a more normal high school experience outweighed my fear of the public schooling system, and for my junior year, I transferred from Cardinal Mooney to Gates-Chili High School. I went from wearing dress clothing to jeans and T-shirts in the blink of an eye. I could suddenly chew gum in the halls, and in the classrooms. They even had a smoking lounge at Gates-Chili. (A disgusting habit I picked up while working at the Diplomat). The culture shock from the transition existed, but I quickly realized, no need for the unrelenting feeling of fear. The shock itself felt freeing and extremely cleansing, like when there is 104% humidity on a day in the high 90s and you step under an icy spray in the shower for relief. Sure, you give a high-pitched scream at first, but then the *ahhhhh* that follows says it all.

With that said, my first day as a Junior at Gates-Chili went nearly as bad as my first day as a Freshman at Cardinal Mooney.

After shopping for all new clothing during the summer, I decided on a slick outfit for my first day as a junior. I purchased a pair of two-tone jeans from Merry-Go-Round. (Millennials and younger may need to utilize Google for an idea of what I am referring to). The front right pant leg was white, the left gray. In the back, the left was white, and the right was gray. I wore a turquoise mesh tank top. (Although I hadn't put on much weight, I had gained muscle from working the last two years). Over the tank top, I wore a gray jacket—one where you could easily push the sleeves up the forearms. (Prime Miami Vice time in society, and the Don Johnson look ruled—again, kids, Google).

Unlike my first two years of high school, I no longer needed the bus for transportation. My hard work allowed me the luxury of purchasing a car when I turned sixteen. I drove to school, WCMF rock music on the radio, and found myself roughly thirty minutes early.

I have been neurotically early for everything all of my life. Even wakes and funerals I never wanted to attend in the first place. It is a curse, but I am unable to change how I am programmed, being *on time* will give me abdominal pains.

The school cafeteria opened early for students craving breakfast, or socialization before homeroom. There may have been some swagger as I walked from the student parking lot, through the hallways, and entered said cafeteria. I thought I looked good, and yeah, I didn't think my shit stunk.

It wasn't as if I didn't know a soul. I knew plenty of kids in the school. I grew up in the town of Gates. Every kid in my neighborhood went to this school. My anxiety pretty much expired, and I felt as if I were home. I had quit my job at the party house and now worked as a cashier at CVS Pharmacy, where Labor Laws were not just observed, but enforced. I had more free time than I knew what to do with.

In line, in the cafeteria, I selected a doughnut and a small carton of chocolate milk. Carrying my tray across the cafeteria floor, I found an isolated table in a corner, sat with my back to the wall, and watched others enter through the doors I had recently entered.

I shook the carton of chocolate milk, smiling, feeling good, feeling happy. I took opposite sides of the carton top and pulled open the top mouth of the milk. I did so with too much vigor, and the chocolate milk protested. It erupted from the giant opening I'd created and splashed down all over my shirt, and jeans.

On the front, white pant leg, it looked as if I had pissed shit onto myself.

I spent the day carrying books slung as low as possible to hide the incriminating stains, head down, chin to chest, praying for the 2:30 bell to ring early, which it did not. In fact, it felt as if time moved slower than normal, and as if on purpose...

Six other people were in my class of new hires. All female. Our instructor had been with ECD for decades and close to retirement. A fantastic person and a great instructor, she loved sharing stories. The first few days we plowed through a thick three-ring binder stuffed full of policies you expect most every company to have, the dress code during the week, and the one for weekends, where you can park (and how to park during winter months), accruing vacation and sick time, calling in sick, requesting time off, zero tolerance when it comes to drug usage, intoxication while working, and sexual harassment. I am sure there were more. Many, many more. I remember feeling like I had just bought a house. Turn a page and sign a document. Initial here. Sign there. Hour after hour. Thankfully, our instructor was awesome at breaking up the monotony with lots of ten-minute breaks.

On breaks, I realized I no longer existed in Kodak's legal department. The environment, a 180 turn from what I was accustomed to, would take getting used to. Especially after signing so many rules and regulations.

The full breakroom reminded me of a saloon. People swore, shouted, and swore some more. It wouldn't be long before I understood things allowed and accepted were completely different and foreign compared to the work environment I had come from.

Bad language never bothered me. Coming from Kodak's legal department, where we handled employment law, it produced something of an eye-opening experience is all. My jaw may have been perpetually dropped in somewhat disbelief for the first few weeks. I knew I would fit in; it would just take some mental adjustment.

I am getting so ahead of myself. I work in a Junior High mentality among my peers, and higher-ups, but realize a simple truth. The childish mentality of Dispatchers, TCCs, Supervisors, Operations Managers, the Deputy Director, and the Director is just the norm. With that said, it isn't every single person. Not by any stretch of the imagination. Just enough people exhibited signs making one (me) wonder if the entire ECD campus could or should be included. Overall, I eventually grow to understand we are all undermedicated people. I say this both lovingly, and with utter frustration. The idea of a communion bowl filled with, instead of hard candies, maybe lithium, carbamazepine, lamotrigine, or any variety of mood stabilizing medications for the taking. Something special for general, liberal consumption, if you know what I mean?

I thought when in the 8th grade, the idea of going to a public high school would be scary. Public high school had nothing compared to the anxiety-, tension-, and stress-filled hallowed halls of the ECD.

As I have said, this is not an exposé about poor management, the union, or *beefs* between Dispatchers. Have there been raised voices, arguments, terminations, bullying, targeting, and gossip? Abso-fucking-lutely. In truth, and though it would take several months before the epiphany crystalized, the people surrounding me at ECD would soon become a second family. It would also become apparent there wasn't anything any one of these people wouldn't do for you or your immediate family, or me and my family. And that you could take to the bank.

Name a non-dysfunctional family, and I will show you a Dysfunctional family. Capital D. (*That's what she said*).

## HOME OF THE GOOD BURGER

The next three plus weeks of telecommunicator training focused on two main things. 1) Memorizing event types, and 2) Practicing taking 911 calls effectively.

There is an event type to encompass any call. The problem is memorizing them, and then knowing which event type to apply to each call.

Let me set the scene for those unfamiliar with how this plays out. (While I am expecting a lot of my readers to be current, former, and/or potential future 911 employees, I hope the reach expands to encompass everyone else, as well).

When a person, let's say it is You—When *you* call 911, the primary goal of the TCC is to get the address of your emergency, verify it, your name, and a good call back number. This way, if the call is disconnected, or something unexpected happens we can start someone your way.

Our script sounds simple. Written out, and practiced, it is. Add the unknown elements: caller is screaming, mumbling, using a crappy cell phone, speaking in an unrecognizable English dialect, speaking a foreign language, or are just so caught up in the emergency you don't answer any of the TCC's questions—and simple, well-practiced rehearsals go down the drain.

The worst thing is when people think all of their personal information populates on our computer monitors as soon as they call. These are people who need to stop watching television because they are incapable of differentiating between fantasy and reality. It isn't how it works. Not exactly. (More to follow in subsequent chapters).

"This is nine-one-one. What is the address of your emergency?"

We don't ask them where they are. That information might prove irrelevant. We want to know where the emergency is. The two places could be one and the same and usually are. Asking What is the Address of Your Emergency, trims the risk of creating an address error.

When my kids were younger, we watched this one movie over and over. Good Burger, released in 1997, starred the comedic duo known as Kenan and Kel. Of course, Kenan Thompson and Kel Michell were their full names, and both are renowned for their humor. The Nickelodeon-produced film, goofy, and ridiculous, is nothing shy of a classic in my household. As I said, we watched it countless times, and I am positive I have it on a DVD somewhere in my house, still.

In the movie, Kel Mitchell portrayed Ed, a behind-the-counter employee at a hamburger fast-food joint. Throughout the movie, Ed repeats a certain phrase. It is said so many times, viewers can't help but laugh.

"Welcome to Good Burger, home of the Good Burger. Can I take your order?"

Good stuff, right?

Painfully, no. In the years I have worked at ECD, the catchphrase, "This is nine-one-one. What is the address of your emergency?" has become so ingrained in my very soul I fear someone might engrave it on my tombstone.

I can hear me, every time I say this, feeling more and more like Ed. I understood Ed better as a character, and as a potential real person after beginning my employment here. Saying *This is nine-one-one. What is the address of your emergency?* now makes me want to stuff grapes up my nose and jump into a strawberry jacuzzi.

At some point, maybe four years ago? The phone system received a much-needed upgrade. We prerecorded the greeting. When a call is answered, the prerecorded message is played: "This is nine-one-one. What is the address of your emergency?"

So, theoretically, TCCs wouldn't need to say the phrase five hundred times a shift. The problem is, more times than not, the caller is screaming at the time of the call, and the prerecorded greeting gets missed. The TCC must then, you guessed it, still regurgitate the stoic hello.

"This is nine-one-one. What is the address of your emergency?"

I hear it in my sleep. Sometimes I catch myself answering my personal phone and repeating the phrase. It becomes, or became, an extension of me in a way I may never be able to shake.

And then there are the event types. We were taught event types ending in an A meant in progress.

Shit is going down right now. The ones ending in a B were for reports, or less important when prioritizing responses.

"There is a car parked on the wrong side of the street."

That is a B all day. PARKB. Officers will get to it when they get to it.

"My girlfriend is an asshole. She hit me last night."

"Where is she now?"

"She's at work."

Also a B. FMTRB—Family Trouble B. If the girlfriend is home, and they are arguing or fighting. Different story. This makes it an A, FMTRA.

"The fire alarm is going off!" First of all, fire alarms don't "go off." But that is neither here nor there. This kind of call is an A. AMTCA—Automatic Alarm.

"There might be someone sneaking around in my backyard." Shit's happening now. SUSPA—Suspicious A.

These are kind of obvious event codes. Not that tough to remember. If kids are smashing mailboxes with a baseball bat, it is considered Criminal Mischief. CRMSA or B (if it happened last night, or a few hours ago).

An ABDCA is someone being abducted.

With just over 130 event types, it felt mind-boggling in class. From a robbery in progress (ROBBA) to a vehicle on fire (VFIRE), there is an event type for just about any and every type of citizen call.

Knowing the difference between robbery, larceny, and burglary is crucial. People will call and say,

"Someone broke into my house. Everything is gone. I've been robbed."

That is not a ROBBA. That is a BURGA—you have been burglarized. A robbery is when you are strong-armed. Your purse has been snatched off your shoulder and the suspect is running down the street. Stealing a case of beer from the local mini mart is not a robbery or a burglary. It is larceny—LARCA.

A crazy driver, crossing the center lines, and running red lights is a RECKLA (Reckless Driver A), but an unlicensed motorcycle or four-wheeler racing up and down the side streets is simply an ATV.

Let's not confuse witnessing someone shooting a gun (SHOTA) to only hearing gunshots (SHOTB), or reporting fireworks in the area (ANOYF—Annoyance Fireworks). Which leads to loud music from neighbors (ANOYB—and only an ANOYA if it is a giant house party, with people spilling out of the house and into the streets).

An appliance on fire, a chimney fire, or smoke inside a house is what we call STRCTB (structure fire), while a house on fire is a STRCTA.

I can review the 130 event types, or you can simply accept me at my word when I tell you there are a lot of things to memorize. The Event Type and its full definition for proper usage when taking 911 calls. For example, when we want officers to check on the welfare of a person (CKWLA), the Cambridge definition reads:

> *A visit made by a police officer or other official person to someone's home [or a specified location] in order to check that they are safe and well and do not have any problems.*

Using the correct Event Type determines the response once the TCC enters the job. Are the police just responding? Police and an ambulance? Just an ambulance? Fire and an ambulance? Just fire? Police and fire? Or are all three needed? The wrong code entered, could give the wrong response.

We used flashcards, broke off into study groups, and I self-studied at home after class. Seemed like it worked well enough. Getting the gist of the events didn't come easy, but I got there. When we utilized offline CAD terminals and practiced simulated phone calls, things started falling into place and started making a bit more sense. The toughest part came from trying to do three things at once. Listen. Talk. Type. All the while thinking—trying to figure out the best event type based on the information the caller shared.

As Telecommunicator classroom training reached the end, we were informed we would all get sent on a police ride-along. I thought this sounded pretty exciting. I have some good friends who are police officers. I asked Mandi, who is a sergeant with the Rochester Police Department (RPD) if I could ride with her husband, Manny, who at the time, also worked with RPD on road patrol.

We were told, before the ride-alongs, we should dress professionally. I had my mother iron me a nice, white dress shirt—wait, whoa. *You laughing?*

I have no idea how to iron. Have is present tense, as in I still have no idea how to iron. I am fifty-two years old (at the time I sit and write this) and to this day I still ask my mother or father, because they are both amazing when it comes to ironing clothing, if they can lend me a hand. And they are thrilled to do so. At least, that's what they tell me, what they assure me.

Not to mention, at this point in life, I lived home with my parents. When my wife and I separated, I moved into a basement, studio apartment. How cliché is that? When we separated, she and I didn't have assets needing divvying up. There was no winter home in Florida, no stock portfolios, or even savings accounts. There were two pieces of shit cars and debt. We added up the balances and divided them by two. She took a handful of cards, and I took a handful of credit cards.

I bought up cheap furniture from Walmart making the apartment far from a terrible place. The kids and I picked out these couches that became beds. Not like they had a bed inside them, but the couch back, when pushed forward, then reclined click-click-clack. The clack meant the down position locked in place, in the bed position. The cushion felt as taught as an army cot and maybe as comfortable as a bunk bed mattress.

The kids and I called them Clickety-clacks. When I picked them up for our weekends together, the three of them would try to shout out first, "I get a Clickety-clack!" As if the piece of junk couch was really something exotic, or luxurious.

By that time, my oldest son was sixteen, Philly. Grant, fourteen. And my daughter, Raeleigh, twelve. Phil usually opted for the leather chair recliner, anyway. I, more than happy having my kids around me, threw blankets and pillows on the floor and slept in the middle of the three of them.

Looking back, it almost sounds as if we spent weekends on camping trips. We'd order food. Stayed up late watching movies. All huddled close as if the tiny apartment transformed into a large tent. I tried, always, making the time together seem fun. In my heart though, it wasn't. I mean, it *was*, I had the best times when I had them with me. But...

You know how on Sunday nights, you start dreading going to bed because when Monday morning comes, you have to go back to work? That feeling crawled inside me and ate away at my very being. It often ruined my mood, making it tough focusing on the present because I already dreaded the idea of returning them to their mother. I never felt like I had enough time with them. My parents always wanted me to fight for more. I didn't want to make waves. My ex and I stunk at communication. We never fought. We both avoided confrontation. Sucky communication probably led to the end of the marriage. I know the root of the end stemmed from our inability to talk to one another. Not to mention, I didn't want the kids exposed to any additional drama. They were resilient during the separation, and I did see them all of the time with baseball, football, dance, cheerleading, and events at school.

The end of my severance pay rolled around about the same time my lease expired. Since, at the time, I hadn't yet been officially hired by the city, I had no choice but to give up the apartment and move back in with my folks. There were child support payments, fees for sports, activities, school pictures, clothing for the kids, and food. The decision became simple.

Besides, *this* is the house I grew up in, which is located off Spencerport Road, in the town of Gates. Being brutally honest? The year I spent alone in that basement studio apartment, I drank a lot, a bit too much most nights. Sat in a dark room with music on and stared at empty walls. I never hung pictures because the basement studio apartment never became *home*. Would never be home.

So I, kind of, embraced the idea of once again living with my parents. They loved having the grandkids over all of the time, too. At thirty-nine years old, my mom cooked me three squares a day. I am not gonna lie, my father did my laundry and ironed my clothing. Was I lazy, or suffering from depression? If I say a little of both, I know I am at least being partially honest.

Dating got kind of weird. Or whatever it was I did at the time with women. Out at a bar, I'd call home. "Hey, Mom? Is Dad up? Is he dressed? Can you get him dressed? No, no, never mind. We'll go to her place."

That never happened. Me calling home first. I knew better. If I tried bringing home some girl I picked up in a bar, my mom would bring in sandwiches, or cake and coffee. You get the idea, right?

Not to mention, I knew things were going to get harder soon enough. Once I finished telecommunicator class, I would get thrust onto the operations floor working a variety of platoons over the next year until I certified as a Dispatcher.

I would be working most holidays. Weekends. Overnights. Not just my life getting impacted here. Not just me stuck in a whirlwind of abnormality. The job would definitely hinder time with my kids.

Holidays. Weekends. Overnights.

This way, at least, while living with my parents I could still get my kids on my scheduled days, and my scheduled weekends, and the kids would be with my family while I worked. The arrangement, far from ideal, still seemed better than the alternative: not seeing them at all.

The day my ex-wife and I sat the kids down and told them we were taking a break, that I would move out for a while, I remember Phil lowering his head. Never said a word. He didn't make one sound. Grant cried, hugging his mom. Raeleigh, who had been sitting on my lap, cried also. There were so many tears they pooled on the hardwood floor beside my feet.

Grant said, over and over, with his voice muffled, because he had his face pressed into his mother's side: "Don't go, Dad. Please. Please, don't go. Don't leave."

I have suffered through this moment in countless nightmares, propelled awake, sitting straight up in bed, eyes wide open and my body covered in a cold sweat. I have never talked about this. Not until right now. My kids are all I have ever cared about.

Anyway, Ah-hem. Where was I?

Ironing.

If you are done snickering about my mother ironing my shirt for the ride-along, I will continue. With my freshly pressed white dress shirt, I picked out a sleek black tie, black slacks, and polished black dress shoes. My—*forget it*. I planned on informing you that my father polished my shoes. I mean, he did, but why mention it?

I arrived at the city police department precinct early, sat in on roll call, helped Manny inspect his patrol car before we headed out, and then buckled up for what I expected to be a wild time.

Dispatched on call after call, one thing became abundantly clear from the get-go.

No matter what type of job we were on, everyone

we encountered addressed me directly. They ignored Manny. Manny wore the full RPD uniform. Gun. Cuffs. Baton. Mace.

But, Manny told me, I wore *the* necktie.

Everyone thought of me as the supervisor. Manny's supervisor. The best part is Manny never corrected anyone. I could see him over a person's shoulder, silently giggling and pointing at me as a woman rattled on and on telling me about the neighbor's dog barking at all hours of the night, every night. She needs a good night's sleep, but it's impossible with the dog always barking.

I did enjoy the ride-along, regardless of my supervisor status. Dispatch sent us on a burglary call (I stayed in the patrol car, while officers cleared the house), we worked our way in on a chase when another officer tried to stop a car for running a red light, and then the car took off as soon as the officer flashed his lights and hit the sirens. That was fun, and a bit scary. My blood rushed, adrenaline kicked in, and I didn't realize how scared I had been until long after I arrived home and thought back on the events of the day.

# IT'S A FUNERAL

As it turns out, in my class of seven trainees, two new hires were picked as Fire and EMS Dispatchers, and two as Police Dispatchers. The remaining three were hired specifically as Telecommunicators. Our instructor informed me I would venture over to, what we call, *The Fire Side*, as opposed to *The Police Side*. Far from thrilled, I figured with my one year of Criminal Justice at SUNY Brockport, and my short career as a paralegal, I'd have been a shoo-in for a Police Dispatcher spot. Even though I knew absolutely nothing about dispatching police cars, I felt as if I knew even less about fire trucks and ambulances.

In the bathroom, during a break, a supervisor told me he'd heard I had been picked as a Fire Dispatcher, and that I had hit the dispatcher lottery. I nodded vigorously, as if I knew what he meant, and hopefully showing him my excitement about such a lottery-winning opportunity.

Dispatching, however, was two months away. I would soon begin taking 911 calls with a trainer for the next month, then back to class for dispatcher training after. I knew enough to know I needed my attention focused on here. Now. Today.

My TCC training took place on 2nd Platoon. Day shift, 0800-1600 hours. Kind of nice, and less disruptive than if I landed on one of the other platoons. Working normal day hours wouldn't interfere as much with my life outside of work. I wouldn't miss much time with the kids even if I worked weekends. Home by 4 PM? I had nothing to complain about.

The only difference between me and the six other new hires? I had been assigned two TCC trainers. I found myself on a split wheel. (Each platoon has three wheels). For my first two days I sat with Tammie, and the second two with Bill. With no clue about who they were, it left me feeling a little apprehensive. Butterflies already flapped about in my gut about stepping onto the Operations Floor, donning a headset, and taking live, *actual* emergency calls.

Like the nerd that I have always been, I armed myself with the given headset, still in its box, the binder from class, and the thick stack of flashcards rubber-banded together. I checked the seating schedule on the corkboard outside the restrooms by the water fountain and saw where Tammie and I would be sitting.

Like a tiny child lost in a giant mall, I stepped onto the Operations Floor and felt my breath catch in my lungs. I actually felt beads of sweat push through the pores in my skin, dotting my forehead. The Operations Floor is something of an oblong, octagon shape. Nearly a third are windows, peeking into the offices of the Operation Managers office, and the rest looked over the atrium—from a different angle, but sharing a similar view as the one from the breakroom.

On the back left side of the room, stood the Police Dispatcher pod. A pod consisted of a grouping of positions. The Police Side consisted of eleven positions. The raised platform in the center, and in a circle, consisted of the supervisor area. On my immediate right, in a large semi-circle—the Fire and EMS Dispatcher pod. There were six positions. Then, scattered in pods of four to five positions, sat the TCCs. There were twenty-one available TCC spots. Not all of them were filled. On weekends, and during the summer, the minimum number of butts needed in seats was higher than during the week, and during the fall/winter, winter/spring months.

Less call volume.

A large domed ceiling bowed above where supervisors reigned. The sound bounced off the almost planetarium-like walls. Whispers from any position in any pod sounded loud and clear below the dome. Maybe not loud and clear. Imagine if the supervisors had us talk to them through empty cans of Campbell soup strung together by wire, or string. Voices had a *tinny* chirp to them, but everything said could be heard, or overheard. The gray walls resembled something found in the recording booth. Not eggshell carton walls, but panels that absorbed and evenly mitigated sound.

Picture twelve TCCs taking emergency phone calls, Police Dispatchers sending officers to family troubles, burglaries, radios emitting static, and beeps and blips. The Fire Dispatchers keying up a full structure assignment for a house fire with klaxon alarms honking, and fire station tones chiming, and everyone talking at once. If you are thinking loud, and chaotic, you would be close.

Concentrating in such an environment took getting used to, an acclimation that didn't come naturally.

Each position, if you'll remember, has an array of computer monitors, keyboards, mice—so many mice. Hanging from the walls are nine television sets. Without sound, and the Closed Captioning on, the sets generally broadcast local and global news. Oftentimes, the "game." Whether it be football, baseball, basketball, or whatever. A few might have soap operas playing during the day, movies, or sitcoms. For the sake of argument, not that I am arguing with myself, but for the sake of argument, generally the televisions were tuned into news channels.

I am not big on descriptions. When I read, the description parts can bore me. I'd hate to have anyone skip over all of the words I so carefully selected, but if you did, I get it. I just wanted to paint a somewhat clear picture (not another sock drawer van Gogh portrait) of the Operations Floor. If you close your eyes, maybe you can visualize the work area. And if you can't perform that task, Google a 911 Center. There have to be pictures posted. The way I understand it, most 911 facilities are set up similarly enough that if you see a few images, and read what I wrote, then we can all be on the same page. Regardless, this should be enough to cover the description. From here on out, I will seriously attempt limiting descriptions that drag the pace of my writing down to something comparable with running alongside a turtle, or a snail (or my little brother Paulie when he is driving. You'd swear Paulie to be in his late eighties and blind, instead of five and half years younger than me).

Now, as I looked around the room, I searched for

the position where Tammie and I had been assigned for the day. Thankfully, placards marked the pods and positions. Seeing the placards meant raising my eyes, and not staring at the floor, or my shoes. I desperately wanted a reason to peer at the Fire Side but kept my head straight.

They all stared at me. I couldn't prove it. I would put money on it, though. You know how you can just tell when all eyes in a room are on you? That was how I felt.

As sheepishly as humanly possible, I shuffled my way toward the back of the room and located the pod with our position for the day. I nodded hello to my pod-mates, who greeted me with smiles. The smiles showed some teeth. I don't believe the teeth were meant to threaten, but instead were a dam for keeping at bay the flood of questions I am sure they were tempted to ask. The grilling would come soon enough once Tammie joined me on the Operations Floor. She was not shy about asking questions. In fact, my trainer got downright abrasive in her teaching techniques. She knows this is true. I even imagine her sleeping with a ruler in her hand at night. Why a ruler? Because when I said or did anything different from what she instructed me to do and say, she whacked my knuckles as if she had been a nun, working in an elementary school from the '40s, reincarnated for the sole, or *soul*, purpose of tormenting me two days a week.

She was intense, but she was also fun, and fantastic to work with (red, cracked, bleeding knuckles aside). And, in between the calls we took, she asked every possible question one person could never have asked another in an entire lifetime, much less in the span of an eight-hour shift.

I listened, and watched, while Tammie took the first few calls of the morning. After the first break, she asked if I thought I might want to jump in the driver's seat and start taking calls on my own. I did not want to do any such thing. I thought my stomach knew how to tie itself into knots before. I was wrong. Dead wrong. For the first time in a long time, I thought I might throw up. The callers this morning sounded nothing like when our TCC classroom trainer simulated calls. The trainer talked calmly, clearly, and concisely, answering every question asked. Real 911 calls, as it turns out, are nothing like simulated calls during training.

---

In the driver's seat, I repositioned the keyboards. Raised the monitors. Took a deep breath, and hit a button making myself available for calls. Tammie's headset was plugged into a shared jack. She could hear everything I heard. She raised the arm of her microphone up, so the caller wouldn't hear her giving me instructions.

I prayed the phone wouldn't ring for the rest of the shift.

A split second later, the phone rang. I felt a part of my anatomy pucker. I depressed the answer button and said for the first time: "This is nine-one-one. What is the address of your emergency?"

The caller was on an on-ramp to an expressway. "The police have the end of the ramp blocked off. Looks like a funeral procession is going by."

I didn't see an issue. "And what is your emergency?"

"Tell the officers they don't need to block the ramp. I have some place I need to be. I can drive in the far right lane. Tell them that. They don't need the entire expressway blocked." The caller gave me a full description of his vehicle. "Tell them to let me onto the expressway. I don't have time for this."

I look over at Tammie. Her eyes are wide like she can't believe the caller is calling with something like this, but then cocks her head to one side, as if saying, Have at it New Boy!

"Sir, I am sure the procession will pass completely by shortly, and regular traffic flow will be restored." It was off the cuff. Made sense when I said it.

Tammie gave me two thumbs up. This wasn't too bad. I could do this.

Except the caller didn't buy it. "I don't think you understand what I am telling you. The policeman, on a motorcycle, is blocking a line of cars from getting onto the expressway. They have shut down the on-ramp, and they won't let me get on. I have somewhere I need to be."

Astounded by the brazen self-importance, I said with a bit of agitated frustration, "Well, sir. As you have told me, it is a funeral passing by—"

*Thwack.* What in the hell was that? A ruler smacked my knuckles. They were innocently posed over the keyboard. Tammie brow furrowed. "You're new, you can't talk to him like that."

She lowered the arm of her microphone, so it sat in front of her mouth.

I'd been tagged, violently so, and she jumped into

the ring. "Sir. It's a funeral. Once they've gone by the on-ramp, traffic will open up."

The caller hung up.

Tammie said, "You handled the caller fine. On your first day, I didn't want you getting jammed up for talking to a caller with sarcasm, yet. Me, I don't care. Not for a caller like that."

Across the pods, I heard someone yell, "Sir, it is a funeral procession."

Tammie and I laughed. Obviously, not happy with how we handled the call, the distressed driver must have called back, hoping for a different outcome.

Callers did that all the time. It happened all the time with wildlife calls.

"We have a bat in our house!"

The different towns and the city, itself, handled wildlife calls differently. In the city, no one responds to bats inside a house unless someone has been bitten.

"I'm sorry. The city doesn't respond to bats in the house. You are going to need to contact an exterminator or check online for information on who can assist you," I have said, too many times to count.

"Are you going to pay for that?"

"I am not sure why I would have to," I answer (Now. Not when new. The getting jammed up thing is far scarier during the first year).

"Well, what are we supposed to do, it is in one of the bedrooms?"

"Is the bedroom door closed?"

So there is no threat of anyone getting bitten by the bat. "Since it is secured in another room, I would suggest calling someone who can help you with this situation."

"Yeah. Right. Whatever." Hang up.

People usually hang up when we can't help them with their emergency. Another common call is for the keys locked in the car. Certain towns will assist residents with gaining entry to a vehicle lockout. The bigger policing agencies will not. Unless your child is locked inside the car as well, and the vehicle is running. When we ask if they have Triple A, or instruct them to call a locksmith, the callers tend to hang up on us. On me.

# THERE IS BLOOD EVERYWHERE

"This is nine-one-one. What is the address of your emergency?"

"There is blood everywhere." Sounded like a young caller, and hard to understand. When she said *blood everywhere*, my stomach twisted into a knot. It was around 1400 hours (2 PM) and near the end of my first day on phones.

"Stay calm." Tammie must have seen my body stiffen.

I readjusted my butt in my chair and sat up straighter. I knew sweat built up immediately under my arms. "Okay, what is the address?"

The caller gave me her location. My mind went blank.

*Thwack!* "Relax," Tammie ordered.

Whacking my hands with a ruler was not a relaxing technique. Not for me, anyway. "Where is the blood?"

"Inside the house."

"Where are you?"

"Inside the house. The blood *are* everywhere." It is what she said.

Blood are everywhere. It didn't make sense. I figured she was nervous.

"Tell her to get out of the house," Tammie told me. "If it is safe for her to do."

Legalese. If it is safe for her to do. Agencies have been sued in the past. A house was on fire. The calltaker instructed the person to get out of the house. The caller was injured exiting the burning structure and sued the 911 department because they had been told to get out of the house. So now we say *If it is safe for you to do so*. Stay. Go. Up to you. No pressure from us.

"If it is safe for you to do so, exit the house," I relayed.

"My jacket and backpack are in the kitchen."

It was December. Cold, snowy.

I already entered the job for the police. A suspicious condition, SUSPA. The text of the job card read: Blood Everywhere. A phrase like that, or GUN, or KNIFE gets attention. She wouldn't be outside alone for long.

"Officers are on the way, if it is safe for you to do so, please exit the house without your jacket." She gets a cold or the flu, and maybe I get sued because I instructed her that she should leave the house without a coat. All calls are recorded. Oftentimes, TCCs are subpoenaed for the purpose of testifying during courtroom trials for a plethora of reasons.

"But the bloods are everywhere!"

*Bloods?* I flashed Tammie a contorted expression. Nose wrinkled. Something wasn't adding up.

"Ma'am, are you saying blood?" It sure sounded like blood this entire time.

"No!" She sounded flustered. "Blood. Blood."

That didn't clear anything up. Even Tammie now seemed perplexed. We'd gotten something wrong. Something missed.

"Not blood?" I kept digging. If it wasn't blood, what were we dealing with? Police cars were well en route. Their sirens blaring. Lights flashing. Blowing through red lights on the way to a potential homicide.

"No," she said. She paused, maybe searching her vocabulary for a comparable word. "Like cockroaches!"

*Cockroaches?* "Bugs? There are *bugs* everywhere?" I asked a clarifying question. She didn't have a lisp, but an obvious speech impediment. I picked up on it at the start of the call. Each word she'd said was a little off. However, I would have sworn I understood Blood was the main factor, the purpose of the call.

Not bugs.

"Yes. They are on the floor and crawling up the curtains."

I let out the breath I had been holding. My sphincter relaxed some. I felt a weight spill off my shoulders. "There are bugs all inside your house."

It was no longer a question. I was stating a fact. This was not a job for the police. "How old are you?"

"Twelve. I just got home from school."

Tammie snatched away the keyboard. She typed: NOT BLOOD EVERYWHERE. BUGS EVERYWHERE!

Police responding 77 (lights and sirens) could slow it down or cancel the job altogether. No one had been stabbed, decapitated, shot, or murdered. The crime scene was nonexistent. No tech job would be needed, no evidence gathered and bagged, and no blood samples taken.

"Okay. What time do your parents get home?" I asked. No longer a 911 emergency, perhaps, I knew the caller still sounded upset and frightened.

"Tell her to have her folks call an exterminator, and hang up," Tammie said.

I didn't want to do that. The girl sounded terrified. I suffered from arachnophobia. Still do. I sympathized with the caller. Creepy crawlies inside the house made me shiver and the hairs on my arm stand on end. I am not a fan.

"They get home at four." Less than an hour until they'd get home.

"When they get home, tell them to call an exterminator, okay?"

"Are the police still coming?"

"They are not," I said, after checking the job. Four officers took themselves off the job. There was no emergency at this location. "Why don't you grab your coat and wait outside for your parents."

"My coat is in the kitchen!" She made it sound as if the kitchen were in another part of the county, and she'd never be able to traverse the distance safely.

"Look, I'll stay on the phone with you. Avoid the bugs, grab your coat, and wait outside."

*Thwack!* "Hang up!"

"You'll stay on the phone with me?" she asked.

I gave Tammie a shrug as if saying, *We've come this far...*

By the end of the call, my twelve-year-old katsaridaphobia had successfully retrieved her coat, navigated a safe path back through the house, and now stood outside waiting for her parents.

I ended the call, a little satisfied with my handling

of the call, despite the folded arms, and stern look my trainer exhibited in my direction.

## MORE CALLS ...

The last call of the shift didn't get much better. "This is nine-one-one. What is the address of your emergency?"

The frantic lady on the other end of the phone gave me the details needed. Small park. Not far from the river. The woman was there with her kids and took them to play on the swings after school.

"Okay, tell me exactly what happened?"

"Ah, there are two gay guys going at it in the park."

I immediately thought it was a fight. A Family Trouble. I pictured two men circling each other. Dukes up. Fancy footwork. "Does either of them have a weapon?"

"What?"

"A weapon? Do you see any weapons? Is either of them hurt?" I asked. "Will they need medical attention?"

"No, I don't think you understand—"

I cut her off. I felt flustered. I needed a police job, and would possibly have to start an ambulance, as well. "Ma'am, you told me two gay guys are going —Ooooh!"

"Yeah, ooooh. Now you get what I'm saying?"

*Now* I got what she was saying. Different kinds of weapons. This wasn't a fight, it was ... *love*.

*Sex*. There. I spelled it out, in case, like me, you still didn't get the subtle innuendo, the implications. I didn't think an ambulance would be needed. Dare I ask for a description of the suspects?

"I let an officer know ma'am, thank you."

VICEA.

How many times could my cheeks burn red? Didn't help Tammie kept her mouth covered, hiding her giggling, the entire time. "You knew what she was talking about?" I asked.

"I knew. I had no idea where you were going with the questions, so I didn't stop you," she explained.

And then, naturally, I started laughing. Snort-laughing. Very becoming on a trainee, let me tell you.

———

And then there was Bill. I trained with Bill on the last two days of my week. Talk about opposites. Although Tammie moved out of state years ago, we are still friends, and still chat now and then (especially since I started writing this book, and I must say, she absolutely agreed with her portrayal...) Bill still is employed with the ECD and is one of the coolest, calmest, and most collective guys you'll ever meet. When I say the man is chill, you can't possibly understand. I am going to do my best, giving you one call-taking example of Bill and me together.

"This is nine-one-one. What is the address of your

emergency?" I ask. The Good Burger scene already replaying over and over inside my skull like tinnitus.

"I want the police here, now. Tired of waiting around for an officer."

"And what is the address, ma'am?"

"I got to give that to you every time I call? Don't that shit just pop up on your screens?"

In movies. On TV. Not in real life. We see the number. A general location. Nothing as specific as to which apartment inside of a high-rise you reside in. "No, ma'am. It does not. What is the address of your emergency?"

A loud, long sigh. Clearly, I am inconveniencing the caller by requesting needed information in order to have police dispatched to assist her.

"Fine," she gasped, as if on the last of her breaths. She fed me the answers needed to verify her location, her name, and the number she called from.

"Okay, tell me exactly what has happened."

This was a real thing. Okay, tell me exactly what has happened. If we don't say that—those words, exactly that way—we get a checkmark for not asking the question appropriately. Leave off the "okay" and you get a check mark. For some reason, *Tell me exactly what has happened* is completely different from, *Okay, tell me exactly what has happened*.

Whatever.

I asked, "Okay, tell me exactly what has happened?"

"My boyfriend has been beating on me. I am tired of him living here."

"Do you need an ambulance?" I astutely asked.

"No, I don't need *no* ambulance? Did I say I needed an ambulance?"

Bill, leaning back in his chair. His hands lay folded just above his lap. In a quiet, softly spoken voice, I barely hear: "Ask her if the boyfriend is there now."

The caller is still yelling, mind you. In one ear, I have her screaming at me. She gave me the boyfriend's name. Age. A clothing description. I am typing away. Trying to get it all down on the job card.

And then, Bill, again. Same softly spoken tone. "Ask her if the boyfriend is there now."

"Ma'am?" I am trying to cut in. Feels as if I am on a feeder ramp, getting up to speed, and attempting a merge into a flow of traffic where there is no break in the long line of cars. "Ma'am, is your boyfriend with you right now?"

"No. He ain't. He out. He won't be back 'til tonight. It's why I am calling, ya'll."

Bill sits forward. "Erase everything you just typed."

That sounded like the most sacrilegious instruction I have ever received. I muted my headset, turning off the microphone so the caller could not hear my discussion with Bill. "You want me to delete all of this?"

"Type, RPT for a report. And then two dashes—"

The caller is on a roll, giving me a detailed description of the misadventures of her recent relationship. I am partly listening to her, so I don't miss anything vital, but also listening to Bill, who insists on speaking in a near whisper.

"—then add half there. Use a fraction. One over the two."

"And that's it?"

"Tell her to keep an eye out for officers. And if her

boyfriend gets home before the police arrive, to call us back immediately."

And that was it? "Ma'am? Ma'am? Ma'am? Ma'am?" I tried.

Bill lowered his microphone. He unmuted his switch. "Ma'am?"

She stopped talking.

"Please keep an eye out for an officer. If your boyfriend gets home before the police get there, call us back immediately."

The caller seemed satisfied. She hung up.

After the call, I asked Bill: "And I just write RPT--½ there."

"That's it." And he moved his hand as if a dolphin rising from and then diving smoothly into the ocean. But in slow motion. I felt my growing stress from the intensity of the call evaporate. "And there you go."

It was a classic Bill-saying. And there you go. *Dolphin-hand.*

Somehow, you just knew, no matter the call, no matter the situation unfolding on the other end of the line. That was it. And there you go.

*Smooooooth.*

# AUTOMATIC FIRE ALARM
## FIRE DISPATCHER (PART I)

# I CAN'T DO THIS

I spent one month on the floor training on phones. The time flew by. The calls never got easier. My experience of listening and typing and talking got moderately better. I learned, for the most part, the easiest way of navigating the CAD mask, ensuring the details of a call got entered correctly.

The CAD mask has dedicated lines for entering an address, the caller's name, phone number, and the details of the emergency.

And now, back in class, three of us newbies would be instructed on the way of Fire Dispatching. Al, both a Fire and Police dispatcher and sometimes acting supervisor, would impart his decades of wisdom to us. Al, a lot like Bill, my TCC trainer, remained very even keel regardless of any situation. House on fire, okay. House on fire with people trapped inside, okay.

The man stayed levelheaded. He knew his shit. Retention became a key component of the job. Retention has never been one of my stronger points (and as I age, I find I don't so much forget things I knew, as much as learning new things has become harder and harder).

The thing about the Fire Side? Shit changed daily.

With thirty-five volunteer and paid fire departments (eight of them also operating an ambulance, as well), the Chiefs all wanted things done in a way specific to their department. And every year when a new chief was voted in (for the volunteer agencies), those policies changed. Naturally, new chiefs knew a way of doing things better, better for them, not better for us.

Each department started its equipment with a number for its battalion. The County, divided into battalions, consisted of five different battalions. The second number on a fire truck was specific to the fire department. The third number might mean the home station for a particular piece of equipment, while the fourth number identified the equipment type. If there was only one station, one home, then the equipment could be made up of just three numbers. But, not always.

For example, Webster Fire Department is in the first battalion. Everything for Webster starts with a one. A Truck/Quint (type of fire truck) will have a Zero, or One, depending. An Engine/Pumper could range from two to five. A Squad ended in a six or seven. Rescues ended in eight.

Ambulances in Nine.

What in the holy fuck had I gotten myself into? Thirty-five fire departments. All with multiple fire trucks. Some with ambulances, as well. I had to memorize five different battalions, which fire departments were in which battalion, and then a battalion that uses six even though they are in the fifth battalion.

The studying became daunting and felt overwhelmingly impossible.

I grappled in class for a handhold.

Al did his best. He taught methodically and rigorously tested us. I struggled to catch on. The numbers became a jumble. My brain couldn't keep them straight. I felt as if I were a dyslexic accountant no one bothered screening before hiring.

Al reviewed policies and procedures. Although I felt accustomed to working graveyard shifts because of my time with Kodak, the idea of sitting in class from midnight until 0800, did not feel like the best learning environment. I won't blame the hours on my inability to pick up on the lessons. I certainly wouldn't blame Al. He taught the shit. Learning it, and memorizing it, fell directly on me.

Al told us about certain locations, where if we ever get a STRCTA, (a structure fire), we should just throw off our headsets, run to our cars and make for Florida, because of the stored chemicals within the specific locations. This included alarms from Ginna, the nuclear power plant just outside the town of Webster, on the southern shores of Lake Ontario.

I wrote it down in my notebook. *Alarms from Ginna. Throw headset. Gather up the kids. Drive for Florida.*

*Got it.*

Around three in the morning (0300), Al had all four of us squeeze into his pickup truck, and we tooled around the city of Rochester. He pointed out the location of every Rochester Fire Department (RFD) house. We didn't stop at a single one. He would just drive by and point. "Engine Five is right there."

Mid-January. Dark as all get-out. "Engine Five is right there."

We're on Lyell Avenue. It's about all I know at the time. I see a small, squat, square building set off the road. By the end of the field trip, I can't remember shit about who lived where. Good deal. But hey, it broke up the monotony of flashcards, dry policies, and endless fire truck numbers.

Back in class, I remember raising my hand. "Al, it says here, RBCST. A Rebroadcast. What does that mean, exactly?"

Words defining a rebroadcast were in the spiral-bound book, but none of the language made sense. Not to me. Turns out, a Rebroadcast was a new event type. Like only days old, new. Al, not sure himself, explained. "When you get on the floor, it will make more sense."

Can I be honest? Once on the floor, it took two months before anyone could explain a rebroadcast efficiently, in a way I could understand. Any time a situation became MORE than what initially thought (fire alarm turned into an actual fire, someone passed out now having CPR performed on them), that was when a rebroadcast was entered. It let agencies know shit went sideways, and in some cases, more equipment and personnel were needed to the scene.

Every morning, after class, I drove home perplexed, exhausted, and out of sorts. Beaten down, I would walk into my mom and dad's house. Of course, they were up. Mom always had breakfast on the table. Eggs, bacon, toast, coffee.

They'd ask like they did every day for the last few months how my day went. My night, in this case.

I am not a talker. I don't communicate well.

Never have. I keep things inside. Avoid confrontation. Avoid exposure to me at all costs. Only a time or two while in Fire Class, I remember telling them how close I felt to losing my job.

"I can't do this," I'd said. "It's too much. I study and study, but I am not getting it."

Al kept saying everything would make sense once we were on the floor doing the job. I doubted him. With every fiber of my being, I doubted him!

And in the blink of an eye, fire class ended with a final exam that I failed. Miserably. Al coached me on answers when retaking the test.

I had the weekend, *my* weekend, which might have been an actual Tuesday/Wednesday, for drinking beer and crying, anticipating my Monday arriving where I would be on the radio dispatching Fire Trucks and Ambulances.

Remember how my sphincter puckered while taking calls? Yeah? Well, that was nothing compared to the way my bowels felt at this point. Too often on my weekend, I came very close to throwing up for no reason other than *my* Monday was now hours away.

It wasn't that I felt unprepared. Trust me, I knew I was unprepared. Lying during interviews at Kodak fell on a different plane. The ability to assemble a machine in no way compared with life and death hanging in the balance. I knew I'd bit off more than I could chew. Somehow, I have built an entire life on lies. Failed marriage. A failed career with Kodak. Now, look at me. My facade, my charade felt close to exposure. Everyone would know I fuck up at every turn but mastered hiding it until this moment.

My Monday would reveal the loser I have always been. The line I'd cast extended far beyond insecurities. I knew reeling in a truth I never wanted to see felt suddenly inevitable. This was a serious job, and I wasn't sure if I was cut out to do it. With the completion of Fire Training Class, the reality of everything haunted my every minute. In moving forward, I would accept responsibility for firefighters and ambulance crews.

My responsibility encompassed their safety from the start until the finish of a call.

Far too often, a trouble breathing call becomes an active family trouble where someone is wildly swinging a machete. I had to be on my best game, all of the time. When updates suggesting a threat to first responder safety showed up on a job card, it was *I* who had to inform my first responders of new, or persistent threats and potential dangers.

Half the time, Dispatchers have no clue about the outcome of most, if any of the calls we send responders on.

We get the beginning. Rarely the end.

I was hours away from beginning a position where my attention to detail, my skills, and an uncanny sense of focus could and would impact the safety of hundreds of people. Their lives, at times, depended on my knowledge, ability, and reaction. Was that not a major mind-fuck, or what?

I was no longer running a machine punching sprocket holes into movie film. Everything about working at the ECD was serious business. Dead serious business. It is literally not a fun and games environment. You didn't take shortcuts on anything. The policies in place (mostly) were there for a reason. And the reasons could be the difference between First Responders going home at the end of their shift, or not.

If the weight of *that* kind of reality didn't make your sphincter pucker, then what would? I couldn't help but think about my little cousin, a police officer, and the dispatcher on the radio the day he was shot in the back of the head.

---

In January 2009, my cousin worked as a Rochester Police Officer (RPD).

He was shot in the head. His life changed forever. I remember, clearly, the day this travesty occurred.

Fourteen-year-old Tyquan Rivera shot my cousin in the head. He was arrested. As a minor, he only spent a few years locked up.

However, prior to working at ECD, I never gave a second thought to Dispatchers. Most people don't.

Think about the reality of this situation. You don a headset. You have some fifty to sixty police officers on your channel. You send them to calls. Family troubles, robberies, and burglary alarms. You check in on the officers once they have been on-scene for a while to make sure they are okay, and then...

A frantic voice pops up and transmits over the air that an officer has been shot.

On scene, the officers scramble. They work to secure the scene, and apprehend the shooter, but also know the officer shot needs immediate medical attention. There's no time waiting for a newly dispatched ambulance. They throw the shot officer into the back of a squad car and speed off toward the nearest hospital.

The dispatcher only has as much information as is shared with them.

As a dispatcher, the prime responsibility, the prime goal, is the safety of our officers, firefighters, and ambulance crews. That's it.

The man on the channel during the shooting of my cousin, never fully recovered. The stress from the flimsy string of details received impacted him. It changed him. He didn't even realize it until weeks, months later.

Dispatchers *own* the safety of the people they send into situations. They take the job as seriously as if they first responded to a scene themselves!

My cousin survived the shooting. His recovery required nearly a year of physical therapy, but it ended with the death of his career with RPD.

# RADIO EAR

I WENT THROUGH THREE AND A HALF ROUNDS OF training as a Fire Dispatcher before certifying. The entire time, touch and go.

At ECD we dispatch for all of Monroe County, including the City of Rochester. The City of Rochester is apart and separate from the rest of the county from a dispatching standpoint.

Let me see if I can break down the Fire Side in a simplistic way. Six positions. There were two designated for RFD only. Channel 1 dispatched the units responding on the job, and Channel 2, what we call the working channel, kept the units updated with details and handled their requests once on scene. Three out of the remaining four positions on the Fire Side were designated to the county agencies, a mix of volunteer and paid departments. The county itself is beautifully split in half, naturally, by the south to north flowing Genesee River. This split by the river gives us the East side of the county, and the West side of the county, each handled by a position on the Fire Side. Both the East and West dispatched jobs on shared Channel 5. The West utilized a working channel, and the East utilized a different working channel. We had a fifth fire channel, that also shared Channel 5, and the westside working channel. This fifth position also served as the break or relief line. The Dispatcher who sat at this position rotated around the pod covering breaks and lunches. And lastly, but not least, was the dedicated ambulance Dispatcher, position number six. They worked on their own channel, and pretty much went balls-to-the-wall from the start of a shift, until the end. The pod, set up in a semicircle, might be considered the epitome of *feng shui*.

On the working channels, a dispatcher becomes little more than a parrot. The officer on the engine, or truck—or battalion chief, or higher-ranking officer on scene—will provide the dispatcher a size-up, an update, or make requests. The Dispatcher, while typing out the spiel, regurgitated everything back over the air, and usually ended with "Okay."

The purpose of parroting let the chief know you heard and comprehend the situation from their side of the radio. Sometimes it goes off without a hitch. In the last thirteen years, I have experienced a good share of embarrassing slips.

My Channel 1 sent an RFD engine to an automatic fire alarm. Two and a half minutes later, the officer on the engine keyed up on Channel 2, where I sat.

"Fire Dispatcher? Engine Sixteen is on location. Nothing showing from a three-story structure. Audible alarms are activated. We'll be investigating."

Nice size-up. Clean, and simple. Right?

I remember wiggling my butt around in my chair, stepping on the foot pedal activating my mic, taking a breath, and while typing, I repeated: "Engine Sixteen is on location. Nothing showing from a three-story structure. You have audible alarms activated. You'll be on vacation."

I immediately shut my eyes. Tightly. In slow motion, I spun around in my swivel chair, hoping no one heard me.

As the newest guy on the team, they listened to every word I said.

Five people stared at me. Mouths agape. "Did you just tell Engine Sixteen they are on vacation?"

"I, ah. I did."

Then Channel 2 squelched. "Fire Dispatcher, we're investigating. Not on vacation."

Oh goodie. I'd been called out on the radio. It took a good half a day before the teasing ended. Though, the blunder will never be forgotten. "Is Engine Sixteen on vacation, Phil" became a thing, and followed me up until even this day. Whenever I do or say something stupid, I can be assured someone will ask the legendary question. I can do little more than arch eyebrows and cringe. It's all in good fun, I suppose. Thankfully, my mix-up of words was not an incident isolated to just me. Every Dispatcher has made similar mistakes, and every now and again, I am sure to remind *them*, as well.

Toward the end of training on the floor, sitting with my third trainer, I was told I would run the entire county for the day. Channel 5, and both working channels. This meant the west of the river, and the east of the river were mine. Departments on the west of the river (their battalions) started with even numbers and east of the river with odd numbers.

Wearing a headset became near impossible as jobs popped up on both sides of the river. I dispatched departments fine on 5. Then they started calling en route on the two different channels. I kept one hand on the mouse for the radios. I needed to toggle back and forth between the different working channels.

Eventually, I had fire departments giving size-ups as they pulled on scene on both working channels at the exact same time.

"Engine Three-Eighty-Two on scene. Residential, two-story house, nothing showing."

"Engine Four-twenty-four on scene, with a person down in the street. We are going to need an ambulance and police to the location."

"Fire Dispatcher, Engine Twenty-nine-twelve on scene with a three car MVA. Start me a trapped assignment. We have an alert patient behind the wheel of one of the cars, but the doors are jammed."

"Fire Dispatcher, Engine One-Zero-Three is on location looking. Can you try a callback? See if you can get us a better location."

My trainer sat beside me. His knees bounced up and down. "Are you going to answer them? We need a rebroadcast for the trapped assignment. We have to start the police and do a callback."

I knew my body became paralyzed moments ago because I couldn't move a muscle. The units were talking on different channels. At the time, I forgot who spoke on which ones. East on this working channel? Or was it West?

"Phil?" he yelled in my face.

I still didn't move.

Then my chair, with me in it, was pushed away from the consoles. My trainer used my headset. He leaned forward and started parroting back information to the different departments on different channels. His hands flew across the keyboards as he got shit done. He called out to another dispatcher to make a call back for the One-Zero-Three's job.

With wrists on my thighs, hands limp between my legs, I knew I'd reached the end. My time with the ECD went as far as it could go.

Once the trainer cleaned up the mess I allowed to accumulate, he waved at a supervisor, had a different Dispatcher take our Channels, and pulled me off the floor. Not literally. He just instructed me to follow him. We went to Secondary Ops, where TCC and Fire Classes were held.

We sat facing each other in the back corner of the room.

"You can't freeze up like that," he said. He spoke in a tone an upset parent used when their kid had done something dangerous, but everyone was okay. "It's why we give you the entire county toward the end of your training. For the volume. It isn't meant to be easy. You are at a point though, where you should be able to handle this. Answer the radio. Answer them all at once if you have to. I know you could have repeated back everything they all said. Then, after that, you get to them what they asked for. Do you understand?"

I did understand, I just felt as if he had more confidence in me than I had in myself. Didn't he know who I was? I am the faker. I have faked my way through life. Keeping up with all of the radio traffic seemed more than daunting. It sounded impossible. I couldn't do the impossible.

I couldn't do this job.

As if he had read my thoughts, he added, "Or you can walk, Phil. If you can't do it, then cut the loss and

PHILLIP TOMASSO

go. Turn in your pass. Because things go to shit out there in the blink of an eye. One second we're all joking around, with little to do, and the next a school bus filled with orphans crashes into a church filled with nuns, and the entire block goes up in flames. You think it was busy just now on the radio? It wasn't. It was like four jobs. The bus hits that church, and it's going to be three hundred times busier. You have to ask yourself if this is the job you want. It isn't for everyone. I can't make that call for you. It's your decision. You take a minute. Sit here. Think about it."

Then he got up and walked out. He left me alone in Secondary Ops. My stomach felt as if it were crushed in a vice, and I might throw up. In my head, I said over, and over. Can I do this? Do I want to do this?

After, around, ten minutes I went back onto the Floor. My trainer caught sight of me from the corner of his eye. I thought I saw a thin smile.

I stood behind him for a moment, while he dispatched on my Channel. When there was a pause in radio traffic, I said, "I'm ready."

"You're ready? You sure?"

I knew everyone in the pod stared without staring. You know how people do that, stare straight ahead but see everything happening all around them? Yeah. They all stared. No doubt they knew every word said back in Secondary Ops. I would surmise some wagering went on, as well. I wonder how many of them bet I'd come back out on the Floor? I really don't want to know who bet against me. I'm sure there were a few of them, too.

"I'm sure."

He took off my headset and handed it over to me. "Well, get to work."

I can't tell you I sat down and dispatched like a champ for the rest of the shift. That would be a lie. I made a shit-ton of tiny mistakes. It didn't play out like a ballerina. Every move made felt clunky, and I took extra steps to get done what could have been executed in an easier fashion. I accidentally put units on the wrong jobs and mixed up words when in parrot mode, but I didn't freeze up. I fixed errors as quickly as I could and managed my channels. I got things done.

About a month later, I actually certified as a Fire Dispatcher. (This meant, after just the one month on phones with Tammie and Bill, I was also TCC certified, even though it had been five months since taking a live 911 call). They brought me to the back office with a supervisor but didn't tell me the reason.

The supervisor had me sign a bunch of papers.

"Are you certifying me?" I asked.

"That's what we're doing."

This meant that when I walked out of the back office, I no longer sat with a trainer. I would Dispatch, and take calls, on my own. I cannot express the fear that was built inside me. I thought my lungs might collapse. I wasn't breathing at the time, so my lungs seemed pointless anyhow.

As we emerged from the back office, everyone on the floor began clapping. My face must have turned turnip-red. I felt my ears heat up as if my cheeks caught fire. I remember thinking, "Oh, shit."

I did know one thing for certain. Getting certified meant a hefty raise, and I could start looking for an apartment of my own!

The certification didn't make me an expert dispatcher. It merely meant I could work independently. I would have questions, would always have questions, and asking the team within the pod is acceptable.

The fire departments would call out with things in a language still new to me. "Fire Dispatcher, we're on scene, hitting a plug."

What *in* the Glory Hell did that mean?

It meant they were making a hydrant, fitting a hose onto a fire hydrant. A long, long time ago, water mains had actual holes in the top of them. Fire departments attached their hoses to the water main. After usage, a tapered wooden plug stopped the water flow, and could easily be removed if needed in the future. It is an old fire-slang-saying. Many still use it. Even the "kids."

"Fire Dispatcher, we're on scene."

Next unit, "Fire Dispatcher, same traffic."

What? What traffic? Are you stuck bumper to bumper on the expressway? Does this mean you are delayed? No. It does not. After the first unit calls on scene, instead of the second unit saying they are on scene as well, they often say Same Traffic. Same traffic simply means "Us, too." Or, we are also on scene.

As I get back to the Fire Side, newly certified and feeling a little too full of myself, I sit on the west. After some congratulations are shared, hands shook, I don my headset and think I might actually shit myself.

About, I don't know, three minutes after that, the guy on the east turns to me. "Did you hear that?"

Huh? "No. Hear what?" I had my radio selected for my working Channel for the west. Someone called out on 5. The dispatching Channel the two of us shared. "What did they say?"

"Start Mercy flight, and get two ambulances going to the parkway, at Lake Avenue. Motorcyclist down. Two patients. Amputated body parts!"

Well, fuck me.

Mercy flight is a phone call. The number is affixed on a laminated card to the wall. My East-side partner grabbed the phone. "I got Mercy. You generate a job and get the fire department, an ambulance and police started that way."

Often, firemen and the like, have a portable radio with them at all times. If they roll up on something, even while off duty, they call out with the information on Channel 5, or Channel 1. Happens all the time. No notice. They rattle off details, and we always need to be ready when this occurs.

I entered a job, adding a police, fire, and two ambulance response.

My partner notified Mercy, and they had a helicopter in the air. Mercy Flight provides air and ground ambulances for treatment and transportation. We have two locations serving Monroe County. Neither in Monroe County. The closest for this particular incident had the helicopter en route from Batavia. The professionals at Mercy are on-call or on standby 24/7.

My thoughts of looking for an apartment vanish. We, as a team, focus on the detrimental situation at hand. The outcome, we learned, did not bode well for the unfortunate people on the motorcycle.

Just certified and baptized by fire as a Dispatcher.

Fun side note. There is both a Mercy Flight East and Mercy Flight West. Each sits on their respective side of Monroe County. They have different 1-800 numbers. If you accidentally dial the first three of one Mercy Flight, and the last four numbers of the other Mercy Flight—it rings up a Phone Sex Line. I won't provide the correct combination of phone numbers. It is an easy enough slip to make, and it has been made at ECD, more than once.

Protip? If you are calling Mercy Flight for an EMS emergency, and they ask for your credit card, hang up. Try again.

## WHO'D YOU KILL LAST NIGHT

For a communications department, sometimes communications sucked. Whether from management to those of us working the floor (oftentimes the case) or between peers. Things got lost in translation. A lot. Too often.

Not long after certification, I moved from Second Platoon (0800-1600) to First Platoon (0000-0800). Midnights. Graveyard Shift. For the record, First Platoon is where I remained. I have no intention of leaving this platoon. I am a night person, it turns out. These are my favorite hours.

Anyway, many of the Fire Dispatchers also worked as volunteer firefighters, and/or on ambulances as EMTs or Paramedics. The people I work with lived the First Responder life. They took every call seriously, as we all should. As we all did.

While on the County East Channel, I sent departments to a house fire. I was about two months in, after certification. The first department arrived and immediately declared a working fire. This declaration prompted a shit-ton of work from the dispatchers. Notifications by way of an antiquated pager system alerted those in "need to know" positions. Phone calls got made. County water. Red Cross. Ambulances are started to the scene, and police are requested for traffic because there are plenty of impatient, self-important people who wouldn't think twice about driving over fire hoses laid across the road.

The chief on scene, in command, wanted a Rescue from a neighboring fire department, and an engine from a different department. It was an odd request based on the job run card. The run card spelled out preplanned assignments for working fires. The Rescue should have come from the second department and the engine from the first. Flustered, the chief on scene may have asked for things backward. I wasn't at the fire. I only followed his directions.

The first department, the one I requested the rescue from, gave me shit. They knew they should be sending an engine. The officer on the radio wanted me to double-check with the chief on scene.

The officer on the radio was a Fire Dispatcher, as well.

I double-checked with the chief, regardless. The chief confirmed on the radio what he wanted. I relayed his request to the officer questioning orders. The officer, on the radio, questioned me. I firmly replied: "Sir, please just send a Rescue as requested. Thank you."

My curt response ended the debate. A house was on fire. Send what is requested. Work it out with the chief after the fire. That was my thought.

When that Dispatcher showed up for work that morning, he approached me. Back stiff. Face contorted in a scowl. "Do you know the difference between an engine and a rescue?"

I did. "I do," I said.

He went on and on, scolding me about what should have been sent.

"I asked for what the chief wanted," I said. I felt completely intimidated by the verbal attack. It was not something I expected. No one in the pod made a sound.

"Yeah? Well, he was wrong."

"Then you should tell him," I said, grabbed my things, and left. I was fuming. I know I was the newest member of the team, but I was forty years old. Who did he think he was, coming into work and giving me a dress-down like *I* was one of his fucking kids?

No one said anything. Supervisors watched it all unfold, and nothing. Want to talk about bullshit?

Things got worse. That night, I sat on the EMS channel, dispatching ambulances. We had several overdoses, and despite doses of Narcan administration, the patients didn't make it. Additionally, a woman with trouble breathing stopped breathing. The Fire Department arrived on scene first, declaring a Medical 500. This meant they were in the process of performing CPR. Once the ambulance pulled up, it was too late. The patient expired. They called a 980 on the air. A 980 is when a person has passed.

The number comes from the Medical Examiner's office. Their vehicle has a number, just like fire trucks, police cars, and ambulances. Obviously, the medical examiner's car number is 9-8-0. So when a person is dead, responders refer to it as a 980.

Send us the medical examiner, in other words.

A pretty rough night, fraught with death. There isn't time while working where one can reflect on the deaths. Generally, this happens later. Usually, on the drive home, or once home and isolated away from the people you do the job with.

In the last ten months, I found myself exposed to unrelenting tragedy and death. It never stopped. It came in waves, or in drips, but it came. It always hit. There were rare days when no one died on my platoon, when a house wasn't destroyed by fire, or a person wasn't shot, stabbed, or raped.

Those were good days.

At the end of this exhausting shift, that same Dispatcher came on the floor. He was my relief. He said as he removed his headset from his handbag, "Kill anyone tonight?"

I lost my shit. I figured he'd been listening to his scanner and knew perfectly well three people died during the night. He wasn't going to let what happened yesterday go. He just wanted to keep it going. Start another argument. Fine. I was not in the mood for his shit.

"You know what?" I shouted.

He sat in the chair I had been sitting in and leaned back with a half-smile, as if saying, *Oh, this is gonna be good*. "No, what?"

"I don't appreciate you talking to me like that." I could feel anger surge like blood through my body. Each beat of my heart forced the anger this way and that way, so all my body could do in response was shake. I hoped he couldn't see the trembling.

"Oh, you don't?" The smile. That half-smile. I could wipe it off his face, and change his expression with a simple...

"Who do you think you are to come in here and

ask me who I killed? I did the best I could on that channnel!"

He shooed me away with a dismissive wave. "You can go now."

"You can't tell me what to do!" Oh, shit. I sounded like a child. *You're not my father*, I might as well have said.

"Ba-bye."

"I'll leave when I want!" I wanted to leave. My stomach swirled in complete turmoil. All four of my limbs quivered. I didn't know if my knees would support me or give up and buckle. "I'm leaving. But because I want to. Not because you told me to."

"Whatever. Have a good day."

Holy fuck! He found my buttons and pushed them. Palmed them! "No. No. I am leaving because I want to!"

His words came in a whisper. I was shouting. Still no interaction from supervision. Hell, I was putting on a free show. I could have sold tickets. Watch me make a total ass out of myself.

I stormed off the floor. I couldn't stop shaking. I had no idea why I let him get to me like that. But he had, and in staying completely calm, he had won. The round. The battle. I was far from done!

Far from done, but there was nothing else I could do.

Outside, as I made my way to my car, my vision blurred by the fury stewing inside my brain, another Dispatcher approached me to make sure I was okay.

We talked for a few minutes beside my car. Slowly, I began breathing more normally, and my spiked blood pressure settled, cooling. My heartbeat no longer slammed wildly behind my ribcage threatening to escape or explode.

"You know it is just an EMS expression, right?" the other Dispatcher said.

"What is?" I asked.

"Did you kill anyone tonight? We all ask it now and then. It just means, was it a bad night, or a good one? Nothing else."

"You do? It does?"

He nodded.

"I thought he was still fucking with me because of the Rescue and Engine shit from the other night."

"I don't think he was. In fact, I think when he came in today and asked you if you killed anyone tonight, it was kind of his way of letting you know the past was in the past."

I asked, "Like an apology?"

He cocked his head a little to one side, as if unsure. "Or his way of saying, let's just get over it."

"Ah," I said, as it dawned on me how much I had blown his question out of proportion. "Well, how the hell was I supposed to know *Did you kill anyone last night* was some kind of twisted term of endearment?"

"I guess you weren't, but you know now."

The next time I saw that particular Dispatcher, I took him aside and apologized. I told him of the rotten night I'd had, and how I had three people die, and I thought he was just picking on me.

We shook hands, he told me not to worry about it. And we never talked about it again.

Until here, and now. In this book. I am not mentioning the Dispatcher, because I still hate myself for this story. For my behavior. The man, to this day, volunteers for his fire department even though he retired from dispatching years ago. Great guy. Big heart. And over the years, he taught me plenty.

God forbid he answered the phone once in a while when he worked, but great guy, with a big heart. Sir, you know who you are. Love ya, still!

P.S.

To this day, I have never asked the person I relieved if they killed anyone during the course of their shift because chances are, someone probably did die while they were on their Channel. No one needs to be reminded of such an event. Especially at the end of a shift, and they might have been successful in pushing away the thought for the better part of their night.

## YOU ARE CORDIALLY INVITED ...
## TO STAY

For the better part of my time at ECD, I worked First Platoon. Midnights until 8 AM. With around eight years left, I don't see myself changing things up. When I first started, and first landed on First Platoon, I couldn't have been happier. The hours fit perfectly in with a single father.

I never had to miss anything. If the kids had an event during the day, I'd go, and then get to sleep in the evening before my shift. If they had something at night, I would sleep as soon as I got home in the morning. I didn't miss holidays with them, or the family (with the exception of New Year's Eve). I rarely missed baseball or football games, cheerleading or dance competitions, chorus or band concerts at school, or school plays.

What I didn't realize was that working midnights I would be perpetually tired, and always searching for a block of time when I could catch a nap, as if I were a junky desperate for my next score.

Staffing the Operations Floor was a numbers game. X number of Dispatchers and X number of TCCs became the minimum. The numbers varied between platoons, which varied with the call volume. (First Platoon incurred the least call volume on average. Another reason why I appreciated my spot on First). When staffing numbers fell below the minimum for the upcoming shift, an employee got "ordered."

Whether it was a Dispatcher or a TCC who got ordered, depended on where the shortage fell.

What is ordered? Let's see if I can explain this in a simple way. Supervisors make a list of employees currently at work. The order list generated is based on an employee's last order date. The most recent person ordered goes to the bottom of the list. The bottom of the list is where you want to be. Those at the top of the list, who had the oldest order date, were then forced to stay and work, potentially, a double shift. The order, in reality, could be anywhere from one to eight hours long.

When I first started my career with ECD, staffing never appeared as much of an issue. If someone needed a day off, the request generally garnered approval. As years ticked by, employees left ECD faster than newer employees could certify. Reminds me of something my father always said about simple finances. You can't spend more than you make. Sooner or later it catches up.

ECD couldn't keep up. The decline in employees, through attrition, became something of a bleeding scab and slowly drained the lifeblood from the body that was ECD. We felt the weakness set in as orders happened more often. Being forced to work doubles takes a toll, not just physically, but mentally, and spiritually, as well.

By the end of COVID (2021/2022), the ECD

sustained anywhere from five to thirteen orders per platoon. Everyday. Every shift. Other than guaranteed Vacation Picks (chosen at the beginning of the year), getting a day off became impossible. Not improbable. Impossible.

Man Workings were the only way to get a day off for a spur-of-the-moment trip, graduation party, or funeral for someone not directly related to the employee. A Man Working was an agreement between two employees, with supervisory approval. "Hey, if you work this day for me, I'll work that day for you."

Naturally, strict rules outlined when, how often, and who could utilize this glorious method for time off, time off that did not tax one's monthly accrued earned time off banks.

Those around me thrived on Man Workings. They buzzed like bees in a dying hive. "Can you work this day for me?"

"When can you pay me back?"

"My schedule's pretty much wide open. I can work for you whenever you want."

"How about next Saturday?"

"Ooooh. Next Saturday? Not good for me. Pick another day?"

"Friday."

"Ewww. Not much better. Other than Friday and Saturday, I am wide open. What else do you need?"

"Monday."

"That's a holiday, though?" Giving up double-time depends on how desperately you need the day off, I suppose.

Yeah. I personally hate Man Workings. It means giving up one of my days off. Sure, I'd get a three-day weekend in return at some point, but a one-day weekend sucked big time. I generally managed my time accordingly. As stated earlier, working First Platoon, I didn't have to miss much anyway. Just had to adjust when I slept. I didn't have money for vacations, so stretches of time off really didn't matter, other than for pure de-stressing and relaxation.

On the surface, it sounded as if life became full of bliss. Everything worked the way it should. For several years, though, sleep avoided me. Too often I stayed awake for over twenty-four hours, and sometimes up for close to forty. It became a regular thing. I sought solace in bed, under covers, eyes closed. Sleep just refused a visit.

You work eight to twelve hours, get home, and try sleeping only to learn your brain can't be shut off as easily as the flick of a light switch. I bought better pillows, higher sheet thread counts, and covered my windows with blackout curtains, all to no avail.

I'd think about jobs I'd dispatched, where I never found out the outcome. What happened to the two-year-old struggling to breathe? Did the person shot in the chest survive the ride to the hospital—a ride with two firefighters on board alternating the performance of CPR in the back of the rig? Did I ever put the ambulance back in service after they went out of service to restock supplies?

A whirlwind of thoughts flashed this way and zipped that way.

I replay call after call in my head, and this keeps me wide awake.

"—there's a dead person in the sleeping bag on the beach. I can see them from my house."

Really, Karen? You see a dead person inside a sleeping bag on the beach? Isn't it more than likely you're upset because someone has camped out on the beach, and you just want them harassed?

But okay. Fine. We'll send an ALS ambulance, the fire department, and a police officer to see what's going on.

Better safe than sorry, right? I mean, I would never *not* send them. The woman calling it in could be right. A corpse might lay curled up inside a sleeping bag, perfectly placed on the beach, just close enough where the soothing sound of Lake Ontario waves lapped only a few feet away.

"Engine Nineteen to the Fire Dispatcher."

"Fire Dispatcher is on, Nineteen. Go ahead."

"Yeah. This is going to be a person asleep inside the sleeping bag. Cancel the ambulance. No medical issue here."

"Any need for the police, Nineteen?"

"No need. We're back in service."

"Okay, cancel the ambulance and police. No medical issue. Just a person asleep inside the sleeping bag. Engine Nineteen, showing you back in service."

Thanks, Karen. Now tomorrow you can call us because your neighbor is roasting marshmallows on a recreational fire too close to the house (and have music, and are dancing, and are having fun, and you weren't invited. And if you're not getting an invite, then you are going to ruin their fun. Calling you Karen might be too nice of a nickname. Maleficent fits the bill).

... And then the next call.

"—Yeah? I live in an apartment above the bar at the corner of this street, and that one?"

"Okay, sir. What is your emergency?"

"There's loud music coming from the bar. It's past midnight. I have to work in the morning. Oh, oh, oh, and there are drunk people in the back parking lot."

You don't say? You rented an apartment above a bar, and loud music and drunk people *surprises* you? You're surprised? The History button on CAD indicates you call every single weekend, all weekend long, for the same thing. Loud music and intoxicated people in the back parking lot.

This, a common call, comes in from unwise tenants who rented tiny apartments above bars on every corner of the entire county. Can't even say, Hindsight's 20/20 because, c'mon, son?

Can I ask, do you mind, what was it you expected when you signed the lease? Expectations couldn't have been that high, to begin with, now could they have?

"Okay, sir. Letting police know the situation."

"You guys say that every time. No police ever show up. And they play loud music right up until two in the morning."

The music stops when the bars close? *Hmmm.* Go figure.

The next call...

"—there's a car going house to house. Pulling into driveways. Then they throw something at the front door of the house. Back out, go to another driveway, and do it again. I'm scared. Send the police."

"Could it be a newspaper delivery person?"

"At five in the morning?" They use a tone like I might be insane for suggesting such a thing. They go on to describe the car and the driver.

I enter a job for the police.

I check the job before my last break. Police arrived on scene. Confirmed newspaper delivery person delivering the newspapers, like he does every morning, seven days a week, for the last two and a half years.

This all runs through my mind, while my head is on the pillow, and for these reasons I believe the idea of sleep teases and taunts me to full awakeness!

Do you know when I feel tired though? After having been up for thirty-five hours? I feel most tired and I would have no trouble falling asleep *right* before the start of my next shift. That's when. Naturally.

---

I can't blame unhealthy diets on rampant Orders. In the breakroom, the one vending machine known as the Wheel of Death, because the inside is a revolving tiered display, showcasing an ill-stocked assortment of expired gas-station-style sandwiches, milk, and cupcakes. Whether here for a normal eight-hour shift or stuck in the building for a full sixteen hours, we are not allowed to leave. There is a classic burger joint across the street from ECD, Nick Tahous. A greasy pit, renowned for its Garbage Plates. Two burgers, or hot dogs set on top of macaroni salad and home fries, covered in a greasy meat hot sauce, onions, and mustard. Can't go wrong with an artery clogger like the Garbage Plate, but if you eat enough of them in a week, a month, or the year, the pants are not going to buckle the way they once did.

Variety was limited unless you planned accordingly and brown-bagged enough food for an entire day of work. Most didn't have foresight.

The creation of Grubhub and UberEats changed the lives of many people at ECD. Suddenly a wave of food—pizzas, Chinese, tacos, burgers, Indian, Thai—lined the counter space in the breakroom.

Names and employee IDs marked bags of food in thick black marker, ensuring the suspected (and well-known) Food Snatchers didn't snatch your food. (We all have food snatchers at work. Those who prowl the refrigerators for snacks, or meals to satisfy their own selfish hunger).

Ordering food daily is expensive. Not *gets* expensive but *is* expensive.

The overpriced, expired food in the vending machines is not the way to go either. I generally believe in boycotting vending machines. A strike against a $5 fee for a twelve-ounce energy drink, or a $3 candy bar. They made it worse when they added charge card / ATM / Easy Pay options. Folks here hit the machines like addicts in line for meth, or gamblers sitting mindlessly for hours feeding a slot machine.

But then again, getting extra snacks from the grocery store is easy enough. So who is at fault? The vendor who charges an arm and a leg for a bag of chips, or the idiot who buys the overpriced bag of chips? I think we know the answer. I may or may not be surrounded by the answer.

The bottom line, generally speaking, but widely speaking—ECD employees overeat. We eat unhealthy foods. We fill our bodies with caffeine, sugars, salts, and fats, then *convince* ourselves that walking circles around the parking lot on break is exercise. Throw erratic sleep into the fray, a brain that replays every troubling call you'd ever taken, and alcohol after most shifts ... Yeah. We're self-destructive at best, and inadvertently suicidal subconsciously, I suppose.

I am a glutton for all of the punishment dished out above.

## YES, WE HAVE NO BANANAS

I RECALL TWO MEMORABLE 911 CALLS, STORIES I enjoy retelling at family get-togethers, and the like. Let's face it. These memoirs would be dry, and a tough read, if not for the salt and peppering of stories.

One day, while at a phone position as a TCC, I took a call that went something like this.

"This is nine-one-one. What is the address of your emergency?"

The caller sounded young. They gave me the address and verified it with the nearest cross streets, their name, and the phone number they were calling from. With everything in order, I moved on to investigative questions. Trying to find out what was going on at the location. "Okay," I said, "tell me exactly what happened?"

Worded perfectly. If this call was reviewed by a supervisor, I could envision the string of Gold Stars stuck to the front of the page, beside my name. (We didn't get Gold Stars, but supervisors did review calls regularly. God forbid we forget to say, *Okay* before *Tell me exactly what happened*).

"I dropped my monkey in the toilet."

First thought, prank caller. Like I said, the person on the phone sounded kind of young. "Is the monkey still in the toilet?"

The other TCCs in the pod looked over at me. I gave them a knowing shrug with both shoulders.

"Yes!" the caller said. They sounded nearly hysterical.

"Take the monkey out of the toilet," I instructed. "Can you do that?"

"Okay. I took him out."

I could hear the splash of water. I imagined my caller holding the monkey over the toilet as beads of water dripped off the fur back into the bowl. I muted my mic and stood up, calling for a supervisor.

"Yeah, Phil?" the supervisor asked.

"I have a caller who dropped his monkey in the toilet. It's out of the toilet now." I had reached a dead end. I wasn't sure where else to take this call.

The supervisor made a funny face, as she made her way down from the supervisor area toward my pod. "Is the monkey breathing?"

I asked, "Is the monkey breathing?"

"No. No, he's not breathing."

I shook my head, and my supervisor's eyes went wide. "Start CPR," she told me.

We used card sets at the time (and now use a computer program, ProQA), for EMS-related calls. I immediately entered a job for the not conscious, not breathing. I noted on the job the patient was a child's monkey that had fallen into a toilet.

I followed the card-set instructions and read them off to the caller. "Listen closely, lay the monkey flat on his back on the floor. Kneel next to him, and make sure there isn't anything in his mouth. Is there anything in his mouth?"

"No. Nothing."

"Okay. You're doing great. Next, place your hand on the monkey's forehead, and your other hand under the monkey's neck and shoulders, then slightly tilt the head back. Put your ear next to his mouth. Can you feel or hear any breathing?"

"No. He's not breathing at all!"

"I'm going to tell you how to give mouth-to-mouth. Completely cover the monkey's mouth and nose with your mouth, then blow two puffs of air into the lungs. About one second for each puff, just enough to make the chest rise with each breath. Can you do that for me?"

I heard him puff, puff.

"Listen carefully, and I'll tell you how to do chest compressions. Make sure the monkey is now flat on his back on the floor. Place two fingers on the breastbone, in the center of his chest, right between the nipples. Push down about one and a half inches with only your fingers touching the chest," I explained. The instructions sounded far too complex for the young caller. Hell, they sounded too complex for me, and I was CPR-certified. If I am in the middle of a crisis, and panicking, someone giving me fractions isn't going to go over well. "Are you with me so far?"

"Okay. Yes!"

Good for him. "Pump the chest hard and fast thirty times, at least twice per second. Let the chest come all the way up between pumps. I am going to count the compressions out loud with you. Okay?"

My supervisor watched me give instructions. She chewed at the corner of her thumb. The others in my

TCC pod were glued to the one end of the conversation.

"Here we go. Ready? One. Two. Three. Four—"

A Fire Dispatcher stood up. "Phil, the fire department is on scene. They are headed upstairs to the bathroom."

"—Twelve. Thirteen. Fourteen."

I heard a door open. The firefighters greeted my caller.

The call disconnected.

I unplugged my headset. My nerves frayed. My hands shook. I had never given out CPR instructions before. This was my first time. The fact that it was a pet monkey didn't matter to me. I felt choked up. I needed to know what was happening. I wished I was on the Fire Side.

The supervisor went over to the Fire Pod. I heard the Fire Dispatchers, and the supervisor laugh. A lot.

"What?" I called out.

"Lieutenant said it was a young man with down syndrome and a stuffed animal. Kid's mother took the battery out of his phone. Fire Department canceled the ambulance and went back in service."

Stuffed animal. I laughed. I laughed, but I also almost cried. My adrenaline raced through my body. The tips of my fingers tickled and twitched.

Years later I took a call that, right from the start, I knew something was up.

"This is nine-one-one. What is the address of your emergency?"

"Listen, listen. Dude. Listen."

I started checking the mapping terminals at the position. See if I could find this guy based on the GPS of his phone. "Can I get the address of the emergency first, please?"

"It's here, man. Right here."

I asked again for the address. He gave it to me. His name. His phone number. "Okay, tell me exactly what happened."

"Look. I just smoked crack, but that's not why I'm calling."

"It's not? Why are you calling?" People called after doing drugs all of the time. Especially edibles. People freaked out on edibles and thought they were going to die. Been there. Done that. Only I wouldn't let my brother call 911. I'd rather have died before letting everyone know I found myself trapped in a time warp. Just kidding. If I really thought I was dying, or if my brother did, he had permission to call for an ambulance.

"Down the alley, alongside my house, there's a gorilla."

A gorilla. That was new. "A gorilla is down the alley? What's he doing?"

"Just sitting with his back against the wall."

"How do you know it's a gorilla?" I had to ask.

"He's got that slicked-back gorilla hair, you know? And those leathery gorilla fingers!"

I put in a job for the police to check the welfare (CKWLA) of my caller, explaining there might or might not be a gorilla down the alley alongside the house.

"Okay, I have the police coming to check on the gorilla. Will you be able to point the animal out to the police when they get there?"

"Yeah! Yeah. I can do that. Tell them I'm sitting right outside on my porch, watching him."

"I'll tell them. You stay safe—"

"Oh, I ain't goin' nowhere. Not with a gorilla on the loose!"

Officers arrived on scene shortly after and asked for an ambulance for the caller. Voluntary Mental Health Arrest.

Oh, yeah. There was no gorilla.

Keeping on with the little animal theme I have going here, I might as well add a third incident. I was on the Fire Side. When I came back from one of my breaks, I checked all the jobs on the screen. It is important to familiarize yourself with jobs entered while on break or lunch, as well as see if your responders are all set on still-open jobs.

One new job card read: "Vehicle is near Angry Goat. Disabled and blocking."

It is a dangerous condition call. We have to make a notify on the Fire Side for some of them. The other type of calls we just let an officer handle.

The job card gave a vehicle description.

I looked at the location. I thought if this had been in the country parts of the county, okay. It was a job for the east side of the city.

I laughed and had everyone look at the job. I said to the group of dispatchers in my pod, "What is disabled and blocking? The Nissan, or the angry goat? And what the heck is a goat doing loose in the city?"

No one laughed. They looked at me like I was crazy. Joe, the Dispatcher on the EMS channel that evening, said, "Are you joking, Phil?"

I told him to go on and take a look at the job. I was dead serious. He said, "The Angry Goat is a pub on South Clinton, and has been there like, forever."

I reread the job card. "Vehicle is near Angry Goat. Disabled and blocking."

A disabled Nissan blocked traffic near the apparently widely known pub, The Angry Goat. Hmm, yeah. That made sense. It made more sense than a loose and angry goat blocking traffic in the city. Didn't mean it couldn't happen. It just meant it wasn't happening right now.

## PURE SHENANIGANS

It was James Howell, who, in 1659, penned the saying: All work and no play makes Jack a dull boy. Perhaps Jack Nicholson made it more modern when he went apeshit psycho in Stephen King/Stanley Kubrick's 1980 rendition of the cult classic, *The Shining*.

Six of us decided, on a day off, that the idea of playing nine holes made sense. On a sunny, cloudless late spring morning we met up at a golf course just off Route 104.

It was my first real taste of hanging out with my peers outside of work. I hadn't realized how essential it was in my search for balance. Naturally, no one could have guessed how sideways a day of dispatchers golfing could have ended up.

What happened? Well, without boring details describing my pathetic swing, the fact I couldn't drive a ball off a tee to save my life, and that I lost more golf balls in trees and ponds than I bought, borrowed, and stole, is beside the point.

We had cold beer, a cool breeze, and golf carts.

While the elite two played ahead, four of us struggled to get anywhere. Matt and I drove around in one cart. Dave and Ryan in another.

It was while enjoying the clean air, which carried a mix of fresh mown lawn and pine trees when things went south, fast.

"What the hell!" I pointed toward the green of the hole Matt and I had just completed. He brought the golf cart to a stop.

Slack-jawed, we watched in confusion the unfolding of unnatural events.

Ryan threw his golf club and yelled, as Dave barreled across the putting green in the golf cart. At the last moment, Dave threw himself out of the golf cart. He hit the ground hard and rolled. The golf cart continued forward, perhaps picking up speed, as Ryan made a failed attempt to get out of its path. Unfortunately, the cart hit Ryan. He fell backward into the golf cart, out the passenger side, and the rear tires ran over his legs.

"What the fuck?" It was Matt who asked this out loud, but I was thinking it.

"I think they're getting attacked by bees."

I was afraid of spiders. That was a phobia. I just hated bees. They were bastards.

"We're going to check it out!"

I didn't want to. I was pretty sure it was a bee attack. Maybe even the killer bees from Africa. They could have made it to New York. It wasn't an unreasonable thought. What was unreasonable was the way Dave and Ryan still hadn't gotten up.

Just as Matt and I arrived, so did the groundskeeper. He rode on a giant lawnmower that looked like something more out of a horror movie than a country club shed. He waited not even a second before chastising the lot of us.

"You kids—"

We weren't kids, though he made me feel like Shaggy, and I wondered if we'd just foiled some dubious and sinister golfing mystery. Not to mention, I remember thinking I could go for a sandwich at the time.

" —racing around doing Batman ... *things*."

That was how he said it. Batman. Long pause. Things.

Ryan, clearly incensed, pointed out the obvious. "Batman things? Sir, I just got run over by a golf cart."

Dave held his side. "I think I broke a few ribs."

Flustered, the groundskeeper pointed at us. He shouted one final warning as he and his crazy lawn contraption did an exit stage left. "Stop dicking around, or you kids are out of here!"

"Dicking around?" Ryan wasn't having it. "I got run over by a golf cart!"

"What the hell just happened?" Matt asked.

Dave fessed up. "My shoelace got wrapped around the gas pedal. I couldn't lift my foot to get it loose, so I yanked my leg back, and fell out of the cart."

"Yeah," Ryan said, "and then I got run over by a golf cart."

Dave had broken a rib, evidenced by his crying as he tried to drive his ball at the next hole and nearly collapsed in total, utter, and near underwear-wetting pain.

Back at work the next night (Dave was out for a few days, and Ryan was bruised as hell), it is rumored Management discussed a new policy. "Six Fire Dispatchers are not allowed to hang out together outside of work if alcohol and golf carts are involved."

We all anxiously waited for the new directive, but it never made it out of the Senate.

———

It was around this time when a complex approved my application, and I found myself moving into a second-floor, one-bedroom apartment. I was moving on up and in leaps and bounds. Little by little I chipped away at the accrued debt my ex-wife and I divided in half and had even managed to put a few bucks away in a savings account. My job as a dispatcher paid well enough. People always complained about wanting more money. I wanted a higher wage too; I had no complaints though. Between my hourly earnings and unlimited overtime, I started to comprehend I had the power to write my own paycheck.

I was past sleeping on a Clickety-clack. The kids and I went on a furniture shopping spree. We picked out a sofa, love seat, and a bedroom set, and then bought a kitchen table from Dave, my friend who breaks ribs golfing.

I'll never forget picking up the keys to the apartment from the main office. It felt as if I had been given access to a whole new world. My life felt as if it were turning around. Maybe not a full one-eighty, but I was getting there. Working tirelessly, and diligently, but getting there, nonetheless.

Shhh. I want to tell you a secret. When I entered the actual apartment I would be renting for the first time (I had seen just models when I visited previously), I saw an extra door. When I opened it, I realized they had rented me a two-bedroom apartment.

I looked at my signed lease contract. One Bedroom. Fixed monthly rent.

Well, shit. Do I tell the front office, or just keep my mouth shut?

Anyway, the next day, the ordered furniture was delivered to my new one-bedroom apartment (*ahhem*) with a spare bedroom, and a few friends from 911 helped me move the rest of my belongings.

The best part of that first night in my new apartment? Making a peanut butter and jelly sandwich in my kitchen. Of course, I had no idea how I was going to get dirty clothes washed and ironed. But I figured I would worry in a week when I started running out of clean underwear.

I still didn't hang any pictures on the walls.


Moving into a place of my own comes with its own rewards, but there is a downside. Remember when I mentioned Man Workings? The only way to get time off is shift-swapping with other dispatchers.

I suddenly found myself in need. On weekends when my kids stayed with me, I didn't want to be stuck working from midnight to eight, or later. I wanted to spend my time with them. I never felt as if I had enough time with them after the separation, to begin with.

Working weekends became inconvenient. I scrambled, ultimately begging people to switch days with me. It wasn't that I wanted every weekend off. Just the weekends when I had my kids. Thankfully, most of the dispatchers helped me out. For many years they helped ensure I got the time off I needed.

A few didn't.

I know who they are. I still won't do Man Workings with them. Spite is a bitter pill I swallow gracefully.

Somehow, I managed to get nearly every day off I needed. It meant I paid a price. Paybacks. I almost never had a regular two-day weekend, but the sacrifice didn't outweigh the benefits I reaped. When I said earlier the people at 911 become family and will bend over backward to help anyone, I meant it.

I worked with some damn fine people.

You need the shirt off my back. Grunts. Groans. Removes shirt. "Here ya go! Pay no mind to my small nipples."

―――――

When my oldest son, Phil—or PT4, as he became known (I am the Third, PT3, and he is, obviously the Fourth)—started thinking about getting married, I convinced him to apply for a job with ECD. He made it through the process, and nearly six years ago began a career working alongside his dad. Me. Sort of.

The funny thing, in his class, was the daughter of a woman who works here as a Police Dispatcher. They put PT4 on the police side, and Morgan (Christine's daughter) on the Fire Side. I suppose they didn't want Father and Son, and Mother and Daughter working side-by-side. I get that. Kind of.

Unfortunately, Phil works Third Platoon, on an opposite wheel. Our days off are never the same. Seeing each other outside of work is very difficult, especially now that he is married, and expecting a third child this winter. (Oh, yeah. Shenanigans don't get more serious than when you consider this guy—two hooked thumbs pointing back at my chest—is a grandfather now. Papa Phil, as I'm widely known by both families, the one at home, and the one at ECD).

My son is not one to be tethered to a workstation. While working as a Dispatcher, co-owned a pizza shop for a brief period, and then bought his wife a bakery. "Something Delicious", in the town of Greece. He even had some claim to fame as he appeared as a six-week contestant on Guy Fieri's "Chance of A Lifetime", and came in second place—missed walking away with his own Chicken Guy restaurant by just a few points!

Regardless, I am proud of him for sticking it out, doing the job, and keeping the safety of our police officers a top priority.

---

I'd be remiss if I didn't point out the love and hate relationship between some fire departments, and some dispatchers. Hate is actually too strong of a word. It is more like love and annoyance. You know how you always love family but don't necessarily have to always like them? It could be like that between firefighters and dispatchers.

I have this one cousin who can do no wrong. He could get caught holding me in a headlock, and viscously grating the knuckles of his fist against the top of my skull, but then tell my mother *I* started it, and *I* would get punished.

Defending myself was always pointless because I

knew my mother would never take my side. My brothers and sisters had my back, but without any authority, that proved as useless as commanding an army of imaginary soldiers. Know what I mean?

(For the record, I don't have a cousin like the one I just described, and my mother is a Saint who knows her oldest son, ME, is flawless in all of the most important ways, eh-oh, oh-eh!)

For the next couple of examples, I am going to pretend that the fire department officers are all named Blah-C-blah-blah. (Just like the equipment, officers have a number structure. The battalion number is first. Then a C. Then the next two or three numbers is their rank in the department). This way I can protect the innocent, and not blatantly reference the guilty (guilty in my opinion).

"Blah-C-blah-blah to the Fire Dispatcher?"

I step on the floor pedal, activating the microphone on my headset. I transmit over the air: "Fire Dispatcher on, Blah-C-blah-blah, go ahead."

"We're on scene with wires down. Can you notify R-G-and-E? We're going to need a crew out here to secure the wires."

RG&E is the local utility company responsible for most of Monroe County. Rochester Gas and Electric. "Will do, Blah-C-blah-blah. Stand by."

I call RG&E. I tell them there is a wire down and a crew is needed to secure the downed wire. They have no estimated time of arrival (ETA). My foot hits the pedal: "Blah-C-blah-blah, R-G-and-E notified. No ETA at this time."

"Okay. Fire Dispatcher can you let R-G-and-E know the wires are live, in the road, and over the top of a car?"

Depress the foot pedal. "Sure, Blah-C-blah-blah. Wires are live, in the road, and over the top of a car. Stand by."

I call RG&E back. Give their dispatcher the additional information. Still no ETA. "Blah-C-blah-blah, R-G-and-E has been updated."

"Did they give you an ETA?"

"Still no ETA, sir."

"Okay, well let them know there is a family of five trapped inside the car under the live wires."

*Mengia Fach!* Are you *fucking* kidding me? Are you on scene and slowly removing one finger at a time from uncovering your eyes? Did you not see all of this right away? I'm a big boy, you can give it to me all at once. *Wait? What?* Disregard (that's what she said).

"Fire Dispatcher, we're going to need R-G-and-E to expedite, please."

*Ya think, dimwit? You could have given me a complete size-up all at once. Make things easier, and then I don't have to call RG&E three hundred times.* Foot slams down hard on the pedal. "Okay, Blah-C-blah-blah. Stand by."

It's frustrating, to say the least. Like when they are on scene for an automatic fire alarm and want us to reach a contact, a key holder who can let them into the structure. We spend anywhere from five minutes to over a half hour exhausting limited resources. The databases fire departments provide for their district are usually so outdated we sound asinine calling someone at three in the morning because they are listed as the number one contact but are curtly informed they haven't been with that company for ten years. Happens all of the time. So we scour the internet, with more firewalls (that should not exist), and finally, tell the chief we were unable to reach a contact.

To which the chief usually replies: "We have a contact on scene, dispatcher. They pulled up right after we did."

Oh, they did, Chief? Did they now? Huh. Sure would have been nice if you let us know. If we were on social media, I would most *definitely* list my relationship status as *It's Complicated*.

---

Dispatching has gotten somewhat better when Fire Departments were kind of strong-armed into revamping Run Cards.

A Run Card appears just before you Dispatch a particular fire department on a particular event. You have to carefully read the entire Run Card to make sure everything gets done correctly (or you know your cousin is going to tell your mom you started it).

Some samples are:


Only Responds Monday - Friday from 0800 to 1600.

Needs an engine/truck from another fire department to go with them.

Will go alone until 0600, but after 0600, and all weekend long will need another fire department to go, too.

Will only respond if the patient is not conscious and not breathing.

Will only respond if there are injuries.

Will only respond for violent psych calls, but not EMS calls unless CPR is in progress.

Will only respond if it is a Waxing Moon on a Thursday, on Odd Months, unless it is summer. Then Even months. But not Thursdays.

Only if Santa Claus personally requests a Fire Response (Tooth Fairy on weekends.)

Hell, there were a handful of departments where if they had a job you knew as the dispatcher the chief would file a complaint regardless of how seamless your dispatch. Sometimes I would scrutinize the Run Card and feel confident I understood the gibberish and unintelligible instructions. Step on the foot pedal, dispatch the job, and then realize, damn! It's not a Waxing Moon. It's a Crescent.

Then I would just yell up to the supervisors: "Hey, can you start my paperwork for event so-and-so, Chief should be calling any second to complain."

Hands to God, nine times out of ten, the phone up at the supervisor area would ring. To no surprise, it would be the Chief. I kid you, not.

We had a guy, who retired not long after I started. We called him Jimmy Buck. He said, religiously, in a mock-fireman tone of voice: "I ain't important at home, or at work, so by golly, I am going to be important at my fire department."

Jimmy Buck was also famous for muttering, "Fuck those fucking fuckers." It caught on. We all mumble the phrase still today. It can be applied to any fuckery that occurs and is acceptable for basic insults if hurled appropriately.

When Police Dispatchers get promoted to Dispatcher II and get certified as a Fire Dispatcher, we tell them. "Be ready to get pulled into the back office a lot."

I am certain the departments and Fire Bureau don't mean anything personal. And yet, I hear the infamous words of Jimmy Buck resound inside my skull, as if sloshing around in brain juice, and spilling out from my ears. Rather than have all of the Fire Departments dispatched similarly they are allowed to have things done differently, and with over thirty fire departments why would any sane person want conformity, uniformity, and structure?

You wouldn't. Make it as chaotic as possible, and then when it gets chaotic because of a storm or multiple fires, you can always blame the dispatcher, wiping clean their hands. A gathered group of pseudo-Pontius Pilates.

It became a thing, at some point, that Fire Departments would ask where their ambulance was coming from when dispatched on an EMS call. They weren't on scene yet, though. So I got in the habit of asking them if they had a patient update for the ambulance crew.

"We're not on scene yet, Fire Dispatcher."

Exactly. How about you get where you are going, and if the ambulance doesn't beat you there, ask us for an ambulance ETA? I know it is fun, and seems important, talking on a radio...

———

I'll never forget one night we got a call for an unconscious student on a college campus. Monroe County has a good handful of colleges and universities. Weekends during the school year are always fun on campus, just not fun for dispatchers.

I started an Advanced Life Support (ALS) ambulance that way. An ALS ambulance has a paramedic on board. A Basic Life Support (BLS) ambulance has a basic EMT.

"EMS Dispatcher to So-and-so. For the unconscious student at (insert location)."

The job was updated. There were now two unconscious students.

I started a second ALS rig that way. "EMS Dispatcher to so-and-so, for the second unconscious patient at (insert location)."

A third update indicated another unconscious student had been discovered. I needed a third ALS ambulance. The agency I just pulled two from was out. I had to mutual aid a second department for the third ambulance.

"EMS Dispatcher, so-and-so to respond with so-and-so for a third unconscious patient found at (insert location)."

The ambulances were all on the way, except my third ambulance driver asked me on the air. "Dispatcher? Why are we the third ambulance to the scene for this call?"

I dropped my foot on the pedal without missing a beat. "Sir, that would be because you were not first, or second."

Lift foot.

Lifting my foot off the pedal in this case felt very much like a symbolic Mic-Drop! Thank you, Rochester. I'm out!

For the record, Fire Dispatchers have the thickest personnel files.

I feel like that could be a bumper sticker, or screen printed on a T-shirt. I know a guy, who knows a guy. Want one? What size?

There is the annoyance of it all. However, the love is much, much stronger. There are no funny story examples for sharing. Instead, it is my admiration for the men and women who volunteer their time to a fire department. Running to calls in the middle of important family get-togethers, and dinners, and when they wake up in the middle of the night to answer the call.

The love I have for my firefighters stems from them entering burning buildings, rescuing people and pets, and doing all they can to save property.

The love I feel toward firefighters grows daily when I see them perform water rescues, ice rescues, and gorge rescues, all while putting their own lives at risk. They are willing to sacrifice their safety to ensure the recovery of a complete stranger.

The love inside me for firefighters far outweighs my annoyance. My respect far outweighs my annoyance. Their continual training and improved response times prove dedication, determination, and drive parallel by no other person, no other group of people that I am aware of.

And just to be clear, I say firefighters. I suppose I should have been more generic, while still being ultra-specific. I mean First Responders. I am talking about EMTs and paramedics. I am referring to law enforcement. These are people who run toward danger. Not away. These are people who care, despite today's wishy-washy media. One day they love First Responders. One day they lead the charge to *defund* this and *denounce* that.

# TEN-SEVENTY-EIGHT

POLICE DISPATCHER

# LET'S DISPATCH POLICE CARS

I SPENT A LOT OF TIME COMING UP WITH PERFECT, or near-perfect section and subsection titles. A 10-78 is a police code. In our county, it stands for a psych call or frequent flier. Someone the police are familiar with because they call all the time for imaginary emergencies.

We had one guy, Willie. He called nightly. If a male answered the phone, he'd hang up. He wanted to talk to the ladies. If it wasn't busy, he would serenade them with some harmonica playing. Frequently, he was intoxicated. Harmless. Everyone knew Willie.

One day Willie called, and the TCC explained it was a busy night and was ready to dismiss him. Panicked, Willie screamed: "But my house is on fire!"

And it was. He ended up moving to Florida shortly after. We all still talk about Willie. Not sure I would classify him as a 78, but he came damn close.

As the section progresses, I believe you will agree it is an appropriate heading.

I took a promotional exam. I felt the time had come to move up at ECD. I scored very well and was slated to become a Dispatcher II. This meant, once certified, I could take emergency calls in a TCC position, dispatch fire trucks and ambulances, and now, also police cars. I was told dispatching police cars was easy. Send one car. Send two cars. Or Ya'll Come Quick—and everyone goes!

After two years, I would be eligible to take another promotional test and become a supervisor. I figured with around ten years to go, I could spend the last eight up top as a supervisor. All I had to do is last two years as a Dispatcher II, and the rest would be easy-peasy, as they say.

What I didn't anticipate is the challenges I would face as a Police Dispatcher. Making things a bit more stressful as I spent a month in class learning how to dispatch police cars, was the fact a new CAD system was in the pipeline. The timing for the change in systems would happen about the same time I would certify as a Police Dispatcher.

This meant spending a month in class learning on "old" CAD, and then three to four training rounds with a trainer on "old" CAD, certifying, and then BAM! New CAD.

Our Old CAD, a COBOL-based system, sounds archaic, and maybe it was, but it is the system I knew and had been working on for years. The New CAD, windows based, would be filled with new, and different commands. I'm an old man at this point. Almost fifty years old. Learning new systems would test my mind and memory. My mind and memory sucked. Little by little my brain worked like a sieve. I retain nothing anymore.

. . .

And just to bring you up to speed. Working as much overtime as I worked, I suddenly found myself in a better situation than I had been when I first started.

As the lease on my apartment approached, an apartment I had been renting for seven years, a co-worker convinced me to start looking at houses. In my very late forties, I couldn't imagine being strapped down with a thirty-year mortgage. I still needed a place to live, and figured, what the hell.

I got together with a realtor and gave her a list of the things I wanted in a house. Single story. Nothing with a big yard. I wanted a postage-stamp-sized lawn to have to mow.

It took some time, but we found a quaint two-bedroom house perfect for me. Even had a fenced-in backyard. Which, after I closed on the property, I knew I needed one more thing.

A dog.

I went to a rescue shelter in a bordering county and brought home a one-year-old Pitbull mix. I named her Ziti, like pasta.

My parents had a dog, Fettuccine. Like the pasta. We called her Fetta, for short. And my daughter had a puppy, one that was all white, and named her Cannoli. Who was I to trample on a new family, Italian heritage, tradition?

Ziti and I are inseparable. She is one of my best friends, and sometimes all I want is to be home with her, watching movies and scratching behind her ear. I started an Instagram page just for photos and videos of my newest family member.

It was almost unbelievable when I realized I was out of debt, a homeowner, and I had a pet dog. I was really living my best life. And with a new promotion, it seemed there was no stopping my forward progress. I was excelling in giant leaps and bounds. Invincible, as they say.

I hung pictures on the walls. Finally.

---

I worked hard in police dispatcher class. Eleven police departments. Each with its own numbering system. And then a numbering system within that system, identifying the police cars. Captains, Lieutenants, Sergeants, Patrol, Detail, Special cars, etc., etc.

I studied. And studied. The instructor did a fantastic job, giving those of us in the class cool and easy ways for keeping the numbers straight. The Rochester Police Department (RPD), the largest working force of the eleven, consisted of five different sections and used the river to divide east from west side cars within the city. They worked with four channels. Two primary channels for dispatching jobs and keeping track of the cars, and two administrative channels (utilized for tow truck requests, calling back numbers, dispatching animal control, parking, checking for warrants, prisoner transports, and anything else officers needed additional assistance handling).

The deputies, Monroe County Sheriff's Office (MCSO), covered the entire county of Monroe. They worked off one primary channel, with two admin channels (one for the east, and one for the west), and shared the air with four of the smaller town police departments. MCSO could, if needed, respond anywhere within the county.

The next big town departments, Greece and

Gates, used their own channel. Irondequoit, Brighton, and Webster were dispatched on another channel. No admin channel, both channels remained very busy with non-stop traffic stops. One after the other, after the other. When the phone rang, the primary dispatcher was responsible for answering the phone and doing the admin work, while also keeping up with the activity on the radio primary.

Don't worry if you can't follow everything I just laid out. It's not easy to explain, and even more complicated to learn as a dispatcher. I put all of the details in here just to give you some idea of the plethora of potential mental roadblocks facing a new police dispatch trainee.

After all these years, that is exactly what I was once again. A trainee. And it didn't feel good. It was downright awkward. Keep my head down, do what my trainer says, and keep on studying even after class ends. There was no watching TV on the floor, reading books, or doing much socializing. I would focus on my channels, and my officers, and not fucking things up too terribly.

I started my training round on First Platoon. Less busy. A perfect way where I could discuss jobs with my trainer between dispatches. For the most part. I fumbled, a lot. With any downtime, I studied classroom materials hoping I'd stay sharp and focused.

The second round moved me from First to Third Platoon. The Third Platoon is by far the busiest of the three platoons. Love it when dispatching on the Fire Side. But the Police Side? Got my ass kicked for an entire month. Two totally different worlds of dispatching. Night and day.

We had to relearn the alphabet. Our county

didn't use Alpha, Beta, Charlie, Delta ... we used names. Adam, Boy, Charlie, David, Edward ... This way, when giving a license plate, or apartment number, it made things clearer.

"Two-twenty-seven, it is going to be apartment 'A' - Adam."

Sitting on the MCSO primary one night, I froze. We had deputies checking for a suspicious vehicle behind a location. On the job card, the caller provided the license plate. The first three letters were HHM and then four numbers. Let's say it was 1234.

Like I said, I froze. I needed to give the plate out over the air. I stepped on the pedal. "Dispatcher to Six-seventeen. You are going to be looking for a white van, license plate"—and this right here is when the brain froze—"Harry ... Harry—"

H was Henry. Not Harry.

I knew I had this wrong. My tongue felt three times too thick for my mouth. I needed grapes, or something juice because my throat became instantly dry.

What in the hell was 'M'?

M is Mary. M is Mary! I just said Harry-Harry, I sure as shit could not follow that up with Mary.

They'd all laugh at me.

So what did I say?

I said, Monkey. I said mother fucking Monkey.

"Dispatcher to Six-seventeen. You are going to be looking for a white van, license plate: Harry ... Harry —Monkey 1234."

I shut my eyes. Tight. My trainer leaned over my shoulder. "Did you just say Harry-Harry-Monkey for a plate?"

"I did."

"I thought so."

And they all laughed at me. I would have preferred packing up my things and going home. I didn't. I stuck it out.

---

One very bright highlight happened while still training. My son and I had primary channels in the city, dispatching RPD. He had the east side of the river, and I had the west.

Any 911 employee, or officer, can check with CAD to see who is sitting where. It will provide the operator/dispatcher/officer name and IBM number, or what we call a badge number.

At one point, both my son and I getting our asses handed to us, sending cars to reports of stabbings, and vehicles into poles, and burglary alarms; sending them to family troubles, overdoses, and panhandlers in the street blocking traffic, a Sergeant called the admin lines and asked: "Do we seriously have father and son dispatching on the primaries?"

The admin told them we did.

The Sergeant asked the admin to inform us that she thought we were doing a kick-ass job and to keep it up.

It was the one and only time my son and I sat back-to-back dispatching together. It is an evening I'll never forget.

---

Police departments all changed shifts at different times. First Platoon cars ended in an A, Second in a B,

Third in a C. The new cars staggered on, and the old cars tapered off. At the beginning and end of my shift, I'd have cars from all over the place.

Police Dispatchers had to keep track of who was almost done with their shift. You didn't want to give them a job. A car just signed on would end up taking the call anyway, but it made you look incompetent as a dispatcher. Or so I had been told, and when I messed up and tried sending a job to a car about to go home, it solidified the lesson taught.

I kept a scratch pad and tried to keep track of shift change times for each vehicle. A logistical nightmare in and of itself. The teachings included knowing who my female officers were, and what car they were in. Were they one badge (patrolling on their own), or two badge (with a partner)?

It had nothing to do with special treatment because the officers were female, but it didn't hurt to keep an eye on them in case a need for backup arose. All the cars listened to every dispatch. They all knew who was going where. And who was in what car? Calling for a car to back another was my job. Officers didn't hesitate to back one another up.

Once certified as a Dispatcher II, and while temporarily on Second Platoon, I dispatched a town police department to an early morning department store burglary. This was a BURGA. Shit going down now. My adrenaline raced. I could feel it like electricity in the tips of my fingers. Cars called out on scene. They then called out as they set up a perimeter around the location.

They wanted K9. I started K9.

A first arriving employee had entered the store.

Saw a guy with a backpack down the front aisle. The employee ran out of the store and called 911.

We didn't know if it was a lone burglar inside, or if there might be an entire team snatching up products.

I handled the burglary well enough. I worked my channel and kept track of my officers.

They sent the dogs in. The dogs brought the man down within seconds.

Police escorted the guy out.

Only it hadn't been a guy. It was a teenager. Just the one. He pretty much got an appearance ticket for court. His father came and picked him up. And the thief got to go home.

No real consequences. This is New York after all. We don't want to hurt the feelings of criminals. Ah, but I digress.

The point being, some days went well. Some I was buried the entire time I worked on the Operations Floor. Buried.

## 10-9

10-9 IN POLICE CODE, IN MONROE COUNTY, anyway, means for the Officer or the Dispatcher to repeat whatever it was they said. For some reason, the radio transmission wasn't clear.

Plenty of officers keep their mic affixed to their dashboards. While driving, they reach forward, depress the key on the side of the mic, and relay a message to dispatch. Unfortunately, that doesn't translate well. They know. They have been told. But they do it anyway. Not all of them, but enough.

"Dispatch, garble-garble gobbly-gook?"

Thankfully, the radio monitor USUALLY shows which car just transmitted. Usually. "Last car, ten-nine?"

"Yeah, garble-garble gobbly-gook."

"Ten-nine, last car."

Then you know, because the officer is frustrated with having to repeat themselves, they have now lifted the mic off the dashboard doc. You know they are holding the mic in front of their face. How do you know? Because, magically, you can understand the words they are saying.

That, or the officer just spit out a mouthful of marbles. This could be what actually happens. I think it is the other way around. They are using the mic the way the mic was designed.

"Dispatch, car-whatever. Out with a stop at X and Y streets."

"Ten-four." We don't parrot on the police side. It came as a culture shock. It took biting my tongue not to regurgitate back exactly what the officer said. The radio traffic on a primary is too busy. Officers have to trust I understood what they said and am typing away attempting to create a job for the traffic stop.

I am geographically challenged, and terrible at spelling. The entire county has some absolutely horrible names. When an officer fires off an intersection for a stop, thankfully I just need to get the first four letters of each street correct, and CAD can verify the location correctly. Old and New CAD.

Getting the first four letters correct wasn't cake.

Hylan Drive vs. Highland Drive

Valley St vs Valley Creek Rd. vs Valley Crest Rd. vs Valley Circle

Aab St vs Abbott St

Wabash Ave vs Wabash St

You get the idea. Many sound alike or have obscure spellings. These are things you don't have seconds to differentiate between.

Because there is a Leopold Street (lee-o-pold), I have heard another dispatcher pronounce Leopard Street as Lee-o-pard Street. We all laugh because we have all done it. And if you are the slightest bit tired, and a job pops up for Saint Stanislaus Street, Rush West Rush Road (say that one three times fast, I double-dog-dare you), Borinquen Plaza—home of the Los

Falmboyanes Apartments (to spit this one out, sometimes you need to square your shoulders and take a deep breath before stepping on the foot pedal to activate your headset microphone). And then Ahepa Circle. Is it ah-heep-ah? ah-hep-ah? I still have no clue.

Anyway, where was I? Oh. Yes. *Immediately* after the officer calls out with the intersection, they proceed with rattling off a license plate number. Using that Gawd-awful alphabet. Too many times I start typing the name, instead of just the letter. Paul David Henry ... I mean, P-D-H.

Now I am behind, typing as best I can to get the correct location to verify. "Car XYZ can you ten-nine the plate?"

I still didn't have an accurate location, and I know I missed the plate completely.

Only, before the officer can key up and repeat the plate, another car, using the same channel, but in a different town, is calling out with an intersection for their traffic stop. And guess what? Rattling off a plate number.

Now I am two plates behind, and I don't have a job created for either officer.

During a traffic stop, I need to get a car to back the officer who initiated the stop. Stops are potentially dangerous, and officers should not approach pulled-over cars alone.

Haven't done that. Yet. I need cars to back my officers. It is a priority.

I am so far behind, though. Yet, it only gets worse. A third car, third town, gives me an intersection for their traffic stop, and a plate.

The first car wants me to run an I.D. check on the driver of the car he stopped.

He still doesn't have a backup. Or a location.

None of them do.

Meanwhile, TCCs are adding (sometimes) useful information to the events they have entered. Every time they hit the Enter key on their keyboard, I get a notification that something new is waiting to be read and reviewed on one of my jobs.

Could be something as important as "...boyfriend just pulled out a gun," or "the suspect is hiding behind the Dumpster in the back of the parking lot," or "the gathered group of fifty people are now all fighting in the middle of the street."

I have to toggle through the updates, see what has been added, and make decisions about what to do about the information. If pertinent, I need to inform the officer responding to that location. If the update just says, "Patient is chewing aspirin" for a medical call, I can care less. Officers won't need that information.

I am, at this point, also not as worried about plate numbers. I am more concerned about getting the stops entered as jobs, so officers in their departments will see the jobs and head that way, even though I haven't yet had time to ask for a back.

A fourth car transmits they just came up on a vehicle rollover. They give me an intersection. They need fire for the person trapped, and two ALS ambulances.

"Dispatch. Have the ambulances step it up. One patient is not conscious, bleeding profusely from the head."

I can't have anyone step it up, because I haven't created the MVAPT job yet, and at this point, I can't recall where the accident even is. "Can you ten-nine the address of the MVA?"

I am frustrating them. I am brand new. Newly certified. The officers don't care. That doesn't mean a thing to them. They need backups and fire departments and ambulances. My incompetence on the channel is my problem, and if I didn't get it under control, it would get even worse. Every transmission dropped me backward down a deeper hole I didn't think I could climb out from.

The officers depend on skilled dispatchers to work their channel. They don't have the time to 10-9 every other transmission. That is not sarcasm. That is the basic, honest truth.

My stomach twists into a pretzel. The dedicated Police Dispatchers I work with do this kind of shit all day and all night long. I was worried I was a breath away from throwing up in the wastepaper basket under my desk.

I don't want to ask them to 10-9 anymore because I feel stupid and completely inadequate. If I don't, though, I can't move forward. Any second another car could call out with more requests.

And then another car would call out with more requests.

It's my channel. I'm supposed to be driving the dispatches. Overseeing officer safety. Getting new jobs out over the air in a timely manner. Only I am not!

I am not. My stomach is twisted, but my heart is crumbling.

It is up to me. I can't have someone else sit down on the channel and clean up the mess I allowed. I have to fix this.

Miraculously, somehow, I do. I can't explain how I caught up, but I did. It wouldn't matter, because, within seconds of the accomplishment, I find myself once again behind the eight ball, with no clear shots in sight.

This is how my time on the police side goes. It begins the moment I sit down at the start of my shift, and never lets up. I miss First Platoon badly. I miss my comfort zone. Everyone reassures me speed comes with time. I believe them. I am just not sure how long I can keep this up, keep letting officers down, and still enjoy my job.

Normally, I signed up for blocks of four-hour overtime spots. Several a week. Work from 2000 (8 pm) to 0800 (8 am).

Once I was moved back to First Platoon, because of staffing shortages, I almost never got any time on the Police Side. Then when I did get assigned a spot on the Police Side, they would stick me in the city, where I was responsible for managing close to sixty cars.

# ALL OUT OF POLICE CARS

New jobs kept popping up in my dispatch windows, despite handling the officers already out on calls. The constant transmissions of intersections, plate numbers, and requests like, can you do a callback, made it near impossible to dispatch new jobs. But, they needed to go out over the air. Air time was precious, and I couldn't snatch a moment to save my life or my career.

What ends up happening too often is that we just run out of police cars.

In a town with six police cars, if three are on traffic stops, and each needs a backup, that's it. That's everyone. The bigger the police force, the more jobs the area endures. Staffing is short everywhere.

When we get the new job for the boyfriend beating up his girlfriend, and I go out with it on the air, sometimes all you hear are crickets. (Not literally. I just mean, no one is keying up their mic to take the job). Traffic stops and family trouble calls are the two most dangerous jobs for officers. More officers are injured, or killed, responding to one of these two types of jobs than any other. I read that somewhere.

My responsibility is to ensure officer safety, such as not sending an officer to family trouble calls by themselves. They have to have a back. Same for traffic stops. When we're out of officers, though, we are out. That's it. You can't get water from a rock, as the saying goes.

If all of my officers are tied up on other priority calls, the girl getting beat by the guy just has to wait until an officer is freed up from their current job.

As a Dispatcher, I sit and stare at the FMTRA, getting updates from the TCC, and know there is nothing I can do to help that woman. Not right at this minute, and sometimes, not for several long, grueling minutes (or longer).

At least on the Fire Side, if we run out of ambulances, we have to keep searching until we find one. Often, we pull an ambulance from a neighboring county. (And when they run out, they call on our crews to assist them, as well).

Not having enough police cars was difficult for me to accept. The *not* being able to do a thing to get anyone started that way haunted me while on the channel, and then during countless sleepless nights. It was not a good feeling, and one I couldn't seem to just accept.

In the city, there are so many priority calls (the event types ending in A), that we can't even estimate when an officer will respond. The jobs hold and hold and hold and hold. They clog my dispatch screen, stacked ten, twenty, and thirty deep with no relief in sight.

When someone is shot, a confirmed shooting, the scene demands a large member of the police force respond. They have to set up a perimeter, start K9, and diligently work to find the shooter. Cars have to block intersections because the area is all potentially part of a crime scene.

And while the police handle a call like that, the other priority calls, still a priority, have to wait until officers can be freed up to respond.

I felt defeated. Deflated had become my norm. It is not a feeling I like. I don't think it is one I can ever get used to, and that realization is nothing short of depressing.

# AGITA

I stopped signing up for overtime. I didn't want to risk working on the Police Side on Third Platoon (from 2000-0000) when I could barely keep up with the police cars on First Platoon. There was no chance I could handle the volume on Third. I am not being modest. I am being painfully honest. Open. Raw.

Making matters worse, the New CAD had a two-month-out launch date.

I was comfortable on Old CAD but could not type and talk half as fast as I needed to when on the Police Side. I just couldn't enter jobs fast enough. I stumbled getting license plates typed out correctly and capturing a car's seventeen-character-long VIN number accurately was near impossible. I couldn't stomach holding priority jobs.

There was no easy way to say this.

The Police Side was giving me *agita*. That's Italian for heartburn, upset stomach.

I called in sick for the last two days of one of my work weeks. I needed serious mental health time off. I had reached a crossroads, and I didn't know which way to turn.

On the long, four-day weekend, I barely left the house. I used the time alone trying to make a list. First I did this mentally. I needed to evaluate the pros and cons of my future as a Dispatcher II.

Then I knew I had to actually sit and write out the pros and cons. It became far too confusing trying to keep it all straight in my mind. Not confusing, really, just seeing it down in ink on paper made it more substantial, and real.

One con stemmed from my loss of money. Sure, I got a nice raise when I was certified as a Dispatcher II. The raise didn't compare to the overtime I gave up though. I was literally too afraid to come in early for fear they would have me on the Police Side on Third Platoon. I couldn't risk it. That was forty-plus hours of overtime a month I left on the table, not some small change.

The new CAD would be out soon. We had a week of training coming up the following month. One full week, forty hours of training on the new system in Secondary Ops. I stole a copy of the training syllabus. I needed to know what was coming down the pike.

I did not like what I saw.

It wasn't that I thought a New CAD would equal a Bad CAD (the jury is still out on that), but I knew it meant I'd be even slower at the job than I currently was. Everyone would be. It wasn't just New CAD for me. It was New CAD for everyone. However, I couldn't envision my speed ever getting up to ... speed.

I worked with these *kids* who just took to everything quickly, and effortlessly.

I started this job at thirty-nine years old. I just made it. I think had I been in my forties, I never would have made it past training. (I have seen many new classes with older people hired for Dispatching or TCC positions, and either before they certify, or shortly after, they quit, or are let go. It is a data dump of information, unique computer systems, unholy multitasking skills, equally downright ungodly attention to detail demands, and many just aren't able to do the job).

It was how I felt now. Dispatching police. Like I just couldn't do the job.

I struggled with a CAD system I knew. How in the hell was I going to be able to do it on a new system?

I know I keep repeating my fear of New CAD. It is something that played over and over in my mind. It weighed heavy on me. I just want the fear clearly portrayed on these pages. Forgive any redundancy.

I think you get it by now, though. I didn't believe I could dispatch police cars on the new system. Bottom line.

The third, and most important thing I thought over while making my list was officer safety.

When I was on a Police Channel, I questioned my ability to keep officers as safe as possible.

Each night when I got home, I thanked God no officers had been hurt while I had the primary channel. I don't think I could live with myself if an officer got hurt because, while I was 10-9-ing the hell out of him, a criminal pulled a gun and shot him.

And I had no idea where they were.

And no one else would know where they were, either.

Why? Because I struggled to get street names down correctly.

Police get in foot chases all of the time. While a Dispatcher II, I never had one. And I am so thankful. When an officer is chasing someone, they call out the streets they pass while running.

Think it is hard to understand them when they are sitting calmly in their car, but their mic is on the dashboard? Try figuring out what they are saying while they scream out streets between huffs and puffs. I have listened to audio playbacks of foot chases. Comprehending the details fired off by the pursuing officer is near impossible for me. The Dispatchers who handle foot chases are gods in my eyes.

And that right there is the key.

That *was* the key.

The Police Dispatchers I work with can do it. They do it. They work their asses off 24/7 ensuring officer safety. Every single one of them takes the job to heart. Any injury, or tragedy, whether an officer-involved shooting or an officer who is shot, they battle with self-doubt and insecurity, questioning themselves, asking themselves if they did everything they possibly could at the time of a crisis.

My hat goes off to the Police Dispatchers. They have my respect, and I am always honored to call them my family.

For me, my crossroads were no longer an issue. Resolve lifted away the yolk burdening my shoulders.

I can easily remember back to when I was first hired, and in the locker room, the one supervisor told me I had hit the dispatcher Lottery when I was selected to be a Fire Dispatcher.

I didn't know what he meant *then*.

I understood what he meant *now*.

About ten months into my promotion, I met with the Ops Manager. An Operations Manager is the layer of management between supervisors and the facility Director and Deputy Director, and liaison with outside agencies. I explained why I wanted to step down. Why I needed to step down.

I gave up the promotion and went back to being a Dispatcher I.

Decidedly, I was able to put away the Pepto and started signing up for overtime again.

I don't think anyone looked down on me for failing. They didn't have to because I have always been my own worst critic. Aside from a fifteen-year marriage, stepping down felt like as big a failure. I couldn't do the job, and it made me feel like shit, embarrassed, and a bit worthless.

I tried telling myself I gave police dispatching a go, it just wasn't a fit for me. That even sounded lame inside my head. Sounded even worse when I said it out loud.

I hadn't been happy, and in fact, I had been making myself sick. I couldn't do eight to ten more years of feeling the way I felt every day until I retired.

Now I would remain a Fire and EMS Dispatcher.

I would never become a supervisor.

I was okay with that.

I knew the Fire Side. In my eyes, I was going back "home." Not some prodigal son, there was no party, no feast welcoming me back. Instead, there was an uneasy silence. No one really asked questions. I sometimes explained the rationale behind why I gave up.

None of those things mattered, though. Whether

they considered me inept or not, I knew the truth. I was inept.

At least, back home, I knew on any channels for *this* side of the room, *my* side of the room, I could confidently work at keeping firefighters and ambulance crews safe in a way similar to how Police Dispatchers handled their officers.

Part of me will always wonder, what if I had been picked out as a police dispatcher from the get-go as I had initially wanted? Would I have made it over thirteenyears as a dispatcher? Would I have been let go, or fired? Sometimes prayers are answered with a no, and we don't know why at the time. Something kind of deep to think about.

We really are the thin gold line on a responder flag. And when polished people are seated in the right positions, man they shine.

Let me tell you, my family shines.

# MORE UNBELIEVABLE CALLS

ONE NIGHT ON PHONES...

"This is nine-one-one. What is the address of your emergency?" I slide a bookmark between the pages of the novel I started reading at the beginning of the shift. I start bringing over information on the caller, trying to pinpoint where he is until he gives me a usable address.

"Yeah. Man? Hey, man? So here's the thing."

I don't want to hear the thing. "Can we start with the address of your emergency, just in case we get disconnected?"

"Yeah. Sure. Sure. But, dude? Can I just tell you what's going on first?"

I purse my lips. "I would really rather start with an address. How about that? Give me an address, then you can tell me what's going on. Sound like a plan?"

"I don't know why you have to be like that," he sounds upset with me.

I believe he forgot he called 911 for help, and by the questions I am required to ask, I can better send the help he needs. But what do I know? "So what is it?"

"What's what?"

"The address of your emergency?" He has a pretty good cell phone. I can figure out, pretty closely on the CAD mapping where he is calling from.

Surprisingly, the man gives me a parking lot behind a building. His location matches what I see on the monitor. I should next ask for his name and a good call-back number. I feel like I would be pushing my luck. I have his location. It is a start. "Okay, tell me exactly what happened?" I ask, keeping my end of the bargain.

"Okay. You see, here's what happened. Exactly." Great. He has dissected my line of questioning. "I just sold these two ladies some weed, right?"

At the time of this call weed, marijuana is not legal in New York. And selling it on street corners still isn't. "Okay?" I ask, hesitantly. For the life of me, I can't guess where he is going with this.

"Yeah? Right? So now, now they won't pay me."

Hmmm. He can't be asking what I think he is asking, can he?

"So what I did, right, is jumped into the back of their car. And I am not getting out of their car until they pay me."

Oh yeah. He is going to ask what I think he is going to ask.

"Wait?" I interrupt him. "So you are, right now, in the back of the car of two women."

"Damn right, I am. I want my money. Weed I sold them was good shit, right?"

"What kind of car are you in?" I enter a VICEA job. I mean, technically, it is a customer trouble. No, no. I can't even type that with a straight face. This caller wants the police to settle his dispute. He feels he has been taken advantage of, and as a drug dealer, he's not going to stand for it.

So he is going to sit for it. In the back of their car.

He gives me a good car description, his name., and the phone number he is calling from. He is making my job so easy now and is quite literally building a case against himself for officers and the courts. Every call is recorded.

I put on the job pretty much everything he told me. Officers will know exactly what they are walking into.

In the pod next to mine, I hear the TCC say, "So this man climbed into the back of your car and won't get out?"

The other half. Looks like the women plan on pinning this all on him. Sad thing is, my caller is too stupid to realize he is going to lose. The women won. They beat him out of a bag of good shit.

I tell my caller, "Officers have been alerted. You keep an eye out for them, okay?"

"Thanks, man. Thanks. Hey, I'm sorry about giving you lip earlier."

I almost laugh. He sounds so sincere. "We're good, sir. We're good." Before I end the call, I add: "Hope things work out the way you want."

I had a sneaky suspicion that things would not end the way this caller imagined.

---

I stayed over to work on Second Platoon one morning. Rochester, New York is not known for experiencing earthquakes. They do happen. In fact, according to volcanodiscover dot com, since 1900, Western New York has been subjected to three earthquakes with a four magnitude, eleven between a three and four magnitude, seventy-two between a two and three magnitudes, and seventy-four below a two magnitude.

One of these small, I am guessing below 2 magnitudes, struck. (Is that what earthquakes do? Strike?) We realized it right away because our calls went immediately into queue.

If we have twelve available TCCs and they are all on a call, and two more people dial 911. We are two calls in queue.

We jumped to nearly fifty calls in queue.

"This is nine-one-one. What is the address of your emergency?"

"I think we just had an earthquake!"

"Okay. Do you need the police, the fire department, or an ambulance?"

"No. I'm okay."

So why in *good God* are you tying up an emergency line? Someone who might actually be in peril is getting a delayed response now.

It wasn't just one idiot calling to inform us of useless information. It was call, after call, for nearly an hour.

"I think we just had an earthquake."

"Do you need the police, the fire department, or an ambulance?"

"No."

Disconnect. No bye-bye. No nothing. Everyone on a phone is diligently at work fielding calls, calling back those who hung up and trying to get responders out to where responders are actually needed.

This sounds funny. It is not. It is frustrating.

People call 911 when the power goes out, too. They call 911 instead of the utility company. Why? I have absolutely no idea. Do they think an EMT is going to climb the RG&E pole in their backyard and figure out what is going on? (Insert Disclaimer: I do not suggest any EMTs or Paramedics attempt climbing RG&E poles. Hell, I don't want to be held accountable for any ambulance crews getting electrocuted on a utility pole).

---

I took a call once for the skunk in the driveway of a caller.

"I can't get to my car," the caller told me.

"Ma'am, skunks live outside."

"Yeah, but I have to go to work. Can you just send the police, please?"

The police? "I cannot."

"You are refusing to send the police to an emergency?" she asked, irked. She didn't even attempt to hide how dissatisfied she was with my customer service skills.

"Do you have an emergency?" I asked, I couldn't help myself.

"I told you already. There is a skunk in my driveway!"

"Skunks live outside."

"You already told me that!"

And apparently, you're not listening. "Unless there is something else, ma'am, I have to take more calls."

"What is your name?"

"Eighty-sixty-eight, ma'am." I am kind. Kinder than the kindest being on the planet.

"I didn't ask for your numbers. I want your name."

"I am not allowed to give out my name, ma'am. My Badge is eighty-sixty-eight, though."

"So you're not sending the police?"

"I am not."

"I'm calling the mayor in the morning."

I wanted to say, tell her I said hello. I refrained. "Okay, ma'am. Have a good day."

"I would, except ... THERE IS A SKUNK IN MY DRIV—"

Disconnect call.

---

Around 0200, I took a call from a lady. She gave me her address, and the other information I needed. I asked her to tell me exactly what happened.

"I can see my daughter having sex through the television. The man is rubbing her nipples. I don't need to be seeing that. I need the police here."

None of them made any sense to me. "Ma'am, is your daughter in the same room as you?"

"No, she's not in the same room with me."

"Is she on TV?" Perhaps her daughter was an actress? A porn star? I didn't know.

"She's through the TV. Through it. And I can see them having sex."

"Is your daughter in the house with you?"

"In the house with me?" She said it in a tone of voice that made it sound as if I were crazy. "No, she's not in the house with me. My daughter ran away."

"She ran away? When did your daughter run away?"

"Almost four years ago."

She was distraught. I had no idea where the daughter was, or if the daughter ran away. What I did know is something was wrong; something was troubling my caller.

I started police that way to check on her welfare.

---

I took another call. It was a frail-sounding older lady. It was the middle of the night. She was crying. She was holed up inside a bathroom. She said someone was inside the house, and she believed she had been kidnapped.

"This isn't my home. I don't live here. I don't know where I am."

GPS put her smack dab in the center of a retirement home. I entered the address from the mapping terminal. It gave me a premise warning. On the warning was the phone number for the nursing staff.

"Okay, ma'am, I am getting you help, okay? Don't hang up the phone."

She hadn't stopped crying. She sounded terrified. She wanted to go home. She kept asking me to save her. "Please, save me. Please, come and save me."

I used the phone next to my position and called the nursing station. They answered.

I told them I had a resident on the line. I gave them her name.

"Okay, we're on the way to help her now. Thank you."

I hung up the phone I used to call the nurse.

"Betty?" I said, "Betty, I have someone coming to help you now."

"You have to help me, please!"

"I'm getting you help, Betty," I assured her.

I heard a knock on the door. "Betty? Betty, are you in there?"

Betty screamed. It was a guttural scream. It made the hairs on my arm stand on end. I just wanted to hug this woman, comfort her, and tell her she was going to be okay.

"I have my walker blocking the door," she told me.

"Betty, I need you to move the walker. Okay? The people on the other side of the door are there to help you."

"You sent them to help me?"

"I sent them to help you, Betty."

The nurse knocked again. "Betty?"

"Move the walker, Betty," I instructed her.

I heard the scrape on a ceramic tile floor. The door squeaked open.

"Hey, Betty. It's okay now." It was the nurse. "Who's on the phone?"

"The police," I heard Betty say.

"Tell them goodbye, now."

Betty said, "Goodbye, I love you."

Out of reflex, I responded, "I love you, too." And the call ended.

# I CALLED 911 ONCE ... ONCE

I LEFT WORK ONE AFTERNOON. THIS WAS BACK when I first started and was newly certified. A couple of Police Dispatchers stood around a car, hood up on a hood stand. I recognized all of them. Paulie and Nick were funny guys. Nick was newer than I was. Jon loved to talk about movies. Matt was the dispatcher I went golfing with, and he had been the one driving the golf cart. I made my way toward my car, climbed in, and drove toward them. Window down, I asked, "What's up?"

"The battery in my car is dead." Nick asked if I had jumper cables. I did. I positioned the front of my car to the front of Nick's. Felt kind of good to help out. I met a lot of people over the months, and this was an opportunity for making new friends. The four of them were Police Dispatchers. I felt as if I were breaking down walls, knocking away cliques. Soon the West and East Berlin wall of ECD would crumble, one battery jump at a time.

I retrieved the jumper cables from the trunk.

Jon, Matt, and Paulie thanked me. "Not a problem," I'd said.

"We'll hook the cables up, and tell you when to start the car," Nick said.

Sounded like a plan. I popped my hood and sat behind the steering wheel. I watched the four of them fumble around through the thin gap between the hood and where my engine sat.

Nick asked, "Is it red to positive and black to negative?"

I climbed out of the car.

"Just kidding, Phil." Nick laughed. Reluctantly, I climbed back into the car. I stared more intently through the gap. I could see them attach the red to positive, and the black to negative.

It didn't matter if red went to positive, and black to negative, as long as the connections matched on both batteries. Just as a "The More You Know" sidenote. At this point, I only saw the connections made on my battery. Part of me felt as if I should say something. Just to ensure the hookup got done properly. The last thing I wanted was to insult them, by suggesting four guys had no idea how to properly hook up jumper cables.

"Okay, Phil. Start 'her up," Jon called out.

I pressed down on the clutch and turned the key. Immediately, sparks shot out of my battery. I saw the ends of the cables burst into flames. I shut off my car and jumped out of the driver's side.

Nick, posed like Hong Kong Phooey (a seventies cartoon character from Hanna-Barbera). Both arms in the air, balancing on one leg, he kicked at the jumper cables. Missed. Switched legs. Kicked again. His foot connected with the cables and knocked one grip free.

As Nick worked on his Martial Arts skills, Jon,

Paul, and Matt paced back and forth saying, "Oh, shit," over and over. Not very helpful.

I dialed 911 on my cell.

A TCC answered, and I immediately became a caller I hated getting calls from.

"This is nine-one-one. What is the address of your emergency?"

"It's Phil. I'm in the parking lot. My car is catching on fire!" I sounded frantic. I have heard the playback after the fact.

"Okay, Phil. What parking lot? What is the address?"

The TCC had no idea who I was. I had not identified myself properly. She didn't know the sound of my frantic voice, or my calm and cool-sounding voice, either.

"I'm sorry. This is Phil. I am a Fire Dispatcher. We are in the nine-one-one parking lot."

"Oh! Phil!"

We didn't have to go through the rest of the questions at this point. I was freaking out anyway. It was a pretty new car, and I didn't want it blowing up.

Nick finally kicked the jumper cables off my battery.

Dave, a now-retired supervisor, came bolting out of the front door. He carried a fire extinguisher. He yelled for us to back away.

The closest RFD fire house was maybe two hundred yards away from ECD. The siren screamed, and the horns honked, as the engine cut through the traffic and pulled into the parking lot.

Nothing was on fire. Other than my cables. Nick stomped out the flames just before the fire engine came to a stop.

Dave gave the cables a squirt from his extinguisher for good measure.

Firefighters investigated the batteries and said everything looked good.

"So, I can use my car?" I asked.

"You can use your car."

I wanted to start it while they were still in the parking lot. They didn't seem concerned, and I didn't want to look like a baby. "Okay, cool," is what I said.

"I'd throw those cables out, though. I've never seen cables that thin. Might want to invest in a better set next time."

"Absolutely," I said as if that were a no-brainer.

The firefighters climbed back up into the engine cab and pulled out of the parking lot. I almost waved goodbye but did not. Instead, I got back into my car. Nick's battery was still dead.

"Sorry," I said, pulling away.

Jon shrugged. "You tried."

"Great karate moves, Nick," I added before my car passed through the security gate.

"Thanks!" I heard Nick call out.

# A WORKING FIRE
## FIRE DISPATCHER (PART II)

# NEW CAD

I talked about New CAD in the last section, but I feel covering the actual time when converted is somewhat essential. Everyone went through a week of training, and eventually, we flipped the switch. Old CAD went bye-bye, and New CAD took over.

The transition went well. The most frustrating aspect of New CAD fell around adding extra steps. While New CAD did basically the same as old, it took two to three more steps to make it happen. The new system can do much more, though. There are more options and more details. It is not a superior CAD by any stretch of the imagination, just a more modern one.

At the time I write this, we have been using the new system for over two years, and the CAD team is still working on fixing bugs in the program. It was a massive undertaking by the team. I can't even pretend to understand all the work that went into the process of designing, incorporating, and executing the switchover.

The one thing I know for sure? I made the right decision by stepping down from the II position. There is not a chance in hell I would have been able to keep up with police requests while using New CAD.

Morgan gets tired of hearing me say things like, "It's just fitting a square peg into a round hole," when I get frustrated with New CAD.

Her take, and she is quite right, is that we are paid to dispatch. It is what it is, so why complain about it? Since she has thrown that in my face, more than once, my complaining about New CAD over the last two years has subsided.

Don't get me wrong. We are usually still hammering a square peg into a round hole but making a fuss about the convoluted system we put in place is as useless as a knitted condom.

*Fuck those fucking fuckers.* (Thanks, Jimmy, for giving me the words to express my overall, and in general, feelings about New CAD).

I would be remiss if I did not point out that the arrival of New CAD may or may not have been directly responsible for an exodus of sorts. Some people retired, some retired early, and some just quit. Many had vocally indicated one of the reasons they were leaving was because, one, they could, and two, they didn't want to have to deal with the new system.

I understand the fear associated with change. Change scares people. The idea scared me. It was needless. For the most part, CAD still works. It just works differently. That's not to say if I had been eligible—or financially secure for the rest of my life—I wouldn't have left, too. Because I would have. In a heartbeat.

Slowly, I watched my 457 and my savings account grow, but not to the point where I could retire. Yet.

## STILL NO NEW POPE

I don't know if winter became one of my favorite seasons because of working at the ECD, or if it is because I am a bit heavy and melt like a round snowman during summer. Either way, winter is the best time for working as a Fire Dispatcher.

The call volume drops considerably from late October until the end of March. From the day I was first certified until today, playing canasta, euchre, Texas Hold 'em, and the like, is how time gets passed between jobs.

We hit this time, regardless of how busy, I consider the Eye of a Hurricane. It is the *calm* between emergency calls. On First Platoon, this is generally between 0430 and 0630. I suppose everyone sleeps at some point. When 0630 hits, the volume ramps up again. There is no actual Distant Early Warning before the flood of emergency calls. No alarm warning us it is about to get busy.

It just happens, and usually, all at once.

People start Waking Up Dead. That's what we say. At 0630 we get a flood of ambulance calls. Dead people are discovered, usually the elderly in nursing homes, or assisted living places.

Until then, we like to set up a card table in the center of the fire pod, and while tethered by headsets to our channels, dealt out the cards. Sometimes we download movies and TV shows onto our tablets. We read books. Many people knit and crochet. Some of the blankets these ladies make are enormous, big enough to cover a king-size bed.

It was a very good fire pod. Morgan and I had City Fire. Morgan, probably one of my best friends, was the dispatcher who started at the same time as my son. K-pop (or Katie), Marcus, Pat, and Josh have the county fire spots, and EMS. Pat and K-pop are on the same wheel. Morgan, Marcus, and I work together on a different wheel. Pat has the most seniority out of the six of us and knows the hundreds upon hundreds of policies inside and out.

Sitting on the primary city fire channel, I know at any point our evening of playing cards could become a whirlwind of chaos with the blaring signal of each klaxon alarm—the sound letting a Fire Dispatcher know they have a new job holding.

Priority calls are red. When you hear the klaxon sound, and see red text on the far left monitor, you know something important is happening.

I hear the klaxon and see a blue line.

I wheel myself away from the card game and pull up into my position. I review the new job that has popped up on my screen. I read the job out loud. "Black smoke in the area."

As I send an engine out to investigate the call, Marcus calls out, "We still don't have a new pope!"

In the Vatican, the papal conclave made up of over one hundred bishops isolated themselves while voting on a new pope. When black smoke is visible no decision has been made. If white smoke, or the "fumata bianca" is seen billowing from the chimney and into the sky, a new pontiff has been decided. There is a new Bishop of Rome!

For Fire Dispatchers, it is kind of the opposite. Plumes of black smoke usually mean something is on fire. Could be from a dumpster. Maybe a vehicle burning in a parking lot. Or...

"Fire Dispatcher." The engine I sent out to chase black smoke. He is on Channel 2, talking to Morgan, my partner in the city. They give her the address. "We have flames through the roof of a two-story residential home. Fill out the assignment. Make this a working fire."

"Working fire, Phil," she repeats, in case I didn't catch it on the radio.

I have sent the working fire assignment. I added several engines, two trucks, a rescue, a battalion chief, the deputy chief, fire safety, and two fire investigators. I dispatch them on Channel 1.

Josh calls out that he has our phone calls. He is going to notify Red Cross and City water.

"I put the weather on the job," Marcus adds.

"I'm looking up owner information," K-pop says.

Patrick adds two ALS ambulances to the job, as well.

The card game waits. We work like a well-oiled machine. Thankfully, it is the only major event taking place. Often, there is something happening in the county, and that ties up those two dispatchers. Right now, the six of us can focus on this one call.

Morgan is transcribing everything the engine announces on the radio. She adds their comments to the job card.

Once K-pop adds the owner information onto the job, I start calling. We are going to need the owner or a representative of the property to respond to the scene of the fire.

A supervisor makes their way over. We have an easel with a map of the city, and points with magnets for where each of the city firehouses is located. The supervisor will coordinate with the Deputy Chief, who is in command at the fire. They need to ensure we have enough engines and trucks—a balance—on both sides of the river.

A supervisor wants me to move one engine from here to there. Just the one fill-in job at this point. As long as things don't get crazy, we can be satisfied the city maintains proper fire protection coverage.

Morgan lets Command know they have reached their first twenty-minute mark. This is important because bottles of air last around twenty minutes. Firefighters inside the structure battling the flames, need reminding. They will fight the fire until the last bit of air is nearly gone. Also, at twenty minutes, Car 99 will conduct a Personnel Accountability Report, or a PAR, which is a visual or verbal count of everyone at the scene of the fire.

Morgan triggers a warble tone. It actually sounds like, Warble-Warble-Warble. "All city companies at the working fire, stand by for par. Go ahead, ninety-nine."

Car 99 checks in with the boss of each engine and truck, getting headcounts. Morgan documents them on the job.

I am on the phone. "Yes. This is the city fire dispatcher. We have you listed as the owner of this property."

It is the middle of the night. I woke them up. "Yes?"

"There is a working fire at the location, we're going to need you to respond, please."

Silence follows. I picture them sitting up in bed, and maybe rubbing sleep from their eyes. "Okay. Give me ten to fifteen minutes. I just have to get ready quickly."

I hung up. "Fifteen-minute E.T.A. for the contact," I tell Morgan.

She repeats it to Command.

The Deputy Chief thanks her. "We're going to need a Red Cross team. Housing for three adults, five children."

Josh calls out. "I've got Red Cross."

The chief continues. "We're also going to need a gas and electric crew to the scene."

Patrick volunteers to call RG&E.

We all hear the next transmission. A firefighter has a victim. It is a dog. He is coming out of the house with the body now.

"Dispatcher," the Deputy Chief says, "we're going to need a Special Services notify. We have one expired dog. The fire is under control. You can discontinue the twenty-minute marks."

The working fire is under control, but we are all brokenhearted. The dog will be bagged and left in a box at the curb for a pick-up in the morning. No one really wants to play cards anymore.

———

City fires run smoothly, most of the time. One to two dispatchers can handle a working fire, even a second alarm fire (an additional two engines, and one extra truck and a lot more notifications) on their own. Even with making the necessary phone calls. County fires are another story.

Rarely will one county fire department respond independently to a fire. Usually, a bordering department will go with them. A working fire may have upwards of four to five fire departments responding.

The radio becomes a cacophony of users talking all at once. Transmissions get covered. Sometimes departments are on an incorrect channel. There are twice as many things that need doing when compared with a fire in the city. The Fire Bureau complicated matters with additional policies and countless notifications to pagers (which have strict timelines for completion, despite the calamity at hand). The fill-ins alone can tie up a single dispatcher. A fill-in is when we move a fire truck from one location to another. Sometimes it is a piece of equipment from the same fire department, but most of the time it is a fire truck from a different department filling in at the now vacant firehouse. And then we have to send a page, so all the chiefs know there is a fill-in. I understand the reason behind notifications, just not within seconds of the move while still handling the fire, answering the channels, and dispatching new jobs. Jobs keep coming in, regardless of what is going on. They don't get put on hold. Slowly, but surely, the deck gets stacked against the dispatcher.

It is essential there exists a balance between the number of fire engines and trucks within an agreed upon distance in an area or town. We do not want to leave any section vulnerable should another fire be called in. Fill-ins help ensure the coverage needed to protect the city and county is intact. The chiefs and ECD Supervisors coordinate the moves, and the dispatchers execute the assignments, accordingly.

Run Cards and a preplanned mutual assistance matrix set the foundation. A chief in command on scene can ask for anything they want. A fire in the county involves a good chunk of the county fire departments. Everyone is going somewhere, whether it is to the scene to fight the fire, to a staging area so they are ready to go to the scene if called upon, or to fill-in at one of the now emptied-out firehouses. Pages need to be sent for each of these moves. And for many, we need actual acknowledgments. We have to mark down who responded to the pages because if certain people don't, we have to call them.

It takes a village to handle a county fire. That is by design, though. Not necessity. (Want to see your personnel file get thicker? Catch a fire in the county. The complaints will follow. It is almost guaranteed).

Don't get me wrong. The city has a person in a role similar to the Fire Bureau, except this person just never seems as hellbent on jamming up dispatchers. The person does, and sometimes for the pettiest of reasons, too. Just not as often. Like, sending an engine 4.5 miles to the scene, because you missed recognizing there was one .3 miles closer. You know, dumb shit like that.

I don't know about you, but I tend to hear the famous phrase once uttered by Jimmy Buck echo, *Fuck those fucking fuckers*, inside my head, between my ears.

We, as fire dispatchers, work hard to get everything done in a timely fashion. We want that fire knocked down and called under control as soon as possible. Residential fires are the saddest. Someone is losing more than their home. The irreplaceable memories, such as photographs, and videos, will be lost forever.

Filling the requests of Command is our priority. We do not want to let anyone down. The pressure is on and stays on until that fire is called under control. You know who has a fire, because they sit facing their terminal, back straight with near-perfect posture, as opposed to slouched over trying to keep their eyes open.

# (CANDID) STORIES FROM THE FIRE SIDE

THERE WAS A FIRE DISPATCHER WHO GOT VERY excited when a job came in for a person who hung themself from the basement rafters of a house. When asked why he looked so happy, he explained he knew the house would go on sale on the market soon. He had been dying to purchase a house in that neighborhood for some time. Pun *absolutely* intended.

Rumor is a Fire Dispatcher once took a 911 call and the person on the other end said they thought their house was on fire. The Fire Dispatcher told them to call back when they were sure and hung up.

---

One night, an ambulance crew had an open mic. They were in an elevator and talking candidly.

"I fucked a fat chick once," the one EMT said.

Their ID was on the radio monitor.

I tried cutting in. "All ambulance crews, please check for an open mic."

They didn't hear me.

"No, it was fun," the EMT could be overheard saying.

I didn't want to call out the actual department. I tried again. "All ambulance crews, check for an open mic."

I heard, "Oh, shit."

It was the same person. I am confident his sphincter twisted into a tighter knot, but the problem was solved.

---

Once, I told a captive audience of dispatchers a funny story. It was about a time, back when I was sixteen. I worked at a bowling alley and met a twenty-four-year-old woman. She bowled in a league. Same night every week. We always kind of made eyes at each other. The flirting went both ways.

I convinced her that at the time I was eighteen. She took me home with her.

She had a three-year-old. She sent the babysitter home and invited me up to her apartment.

Before we did anything inappropriate, the lady gave her child a snack, and we all watched some cartoons.

The child sat in a wicker rocking chair and just stared at me singing an LL Cool J song. "I'm going back to Cali, Cali, Cali. I'm going back to Cali, nah, I don't think so."

I am singing the song, so everyone gets an idea of how it goes. It is an older tune, and pretty much none of them had ever heard it before.

I explained all of this, and then the phone rang in the tiny apartment. The child answered it.

"Oh, nothing," she said, still staring at me.

Her mother kept reaching for the phone. (This is before cell phones. But it was cordless, with a pull-up antenna). The child twisted and turned, escaping her mother's grasp. "Phil's here," she told the caller.

Her father.

The woman's ex-boyfriend.

I clapped a hand to my own forehead, exasperated all over again when our phone at work rang. It was one of the ambulance bases.

We had an open mic, and my sexcapade had been transmitted crisply, and clearly, across Monroe County.

I wanted to go to Cali, Cali, Cali, let me tell you right now.

I have learned, always check to see if a mic is active before you say anything you wouldn't want the rest of the community hearing.

# SOME CALLS YOU JUST NEVER FORGET

A woman called. Said she lived on a street at a house she rented, where it was the only house on the street without a driveway. Every other house on the street had a driveway.

"Okay, ma'am. Tell me exactly what happened?" I asked.

"That's what I am trying to do."

"Okay, I'm listening."

"I talked to my neighbors about not parking on the street in front of my house, because it forces me to have to find alternate parking, sometimes as far as a block and a half away from where I live," she said. She made it sound, by her tone of voice, as if she were making a serious point, and that I should be following her narrative. She continued. "When I have groceries, or I am tired after getting home from work, it makes for a long walk. And I shouldn't have to park two blocks away from where I live. Do you understand?"

I did understand. Sounded as if it sucked big time. I just wasn't sure why she was calling 911. I asked her, "What is the issue tonight, ma'am?"

"Well, it looks like a few of the houses on the block are having a party."

It's summertime. End of June. Graduations and weddings are in full swing. I didn't doubt there was some celebration taking place around the entire county.

"There are cars parked on the street, in front of my house. Up and down both sides of the road." She wanted the police to come and handle the situation.

I asked, "Handle what situation?"

"Have you not been listening to me?"

"No, ma'am. I have been listening. I am just not sure what the issue is."

She repeated how she had already talked with neighbors about respecting the space on the street in front of her house, and now they had blatantly ignored her request.

"Ma'am," I explained, "parking on the street, where parking is permitted, is not a police matter. It is legal."

"I just *can't* with people in New York. This would never fly in the south," she informed me. She said, "Now where am I supposed to park?"

I asked her, "Ma'am, when you rented out the house did you realize you did not have a driveway, and that you would be parking in the street?"

She said, "I already told you I had the situation handled. Everyone agreed to respect the spot in front of my house."

I asked again, "Well, regardless, did you know it did not have a driveway?"

"That's not the point. You are very rude!" She hung up.

And I, I shook my head, feeling sorry for those neighbors come morning.

---

While not a specific call example, this is the type of call I, and every other TCC, take regularly.

"This is nine-one-one. What is the address of your emergency?"

"Can you send the police right away?" Female caller. Four in the morning.

Once I get an address, her name, and her phone number. "Okay, tell me exactly what happened?"

"My baby-daddy is here, and he won't leave."

"Is there any alcohol or drugs involved?"

"We been drinking."

"Does he have any weapons?"

"I don't know." Her tone of voice is flat.

"Did you see any weapons?"

"I don't know." She is non-engaged.

"Are there any diagnosed mental health issues?"

"I don't know." It sounds as if she is bored or watching TV, instead of calling 911 for an emergency.

"Are there any orders of protection in place?"

"Yeah, I got one against him."

But they had been drinking together.

"What's his name?"

"I don't know." The monotone answers begin to annoy me.

"He's the father of your child, and you don't know his name?"

"Nope." She enunciates the "p" in nope, almost as if giving me a big ho-hum.

"And he's been over there drinking with you, and you never asked his name?"

"Nope." There it is again. The over-annunciated "p."

"What's he wearing?"

"I don't know."

"Where is he?"

"Sitting on the couch next to me," she says, flatly.

It is a game. Happens all the time. The caller is fed up with her visitor and calling 911 to scare them into leaving is how they handle their relationships. It is a power trip. Someone showing someone else who has the upper hand. They use 911 as the vehicle. She isn't going to press charges. More than likely, he hasn't done a thing wrong, other than violate an order of protection, that she probably voided when she invited him over for drinks.

I document all of the information on the job card, and enter an FMTRA, frustrated that we are going to waste and tie up police resources for this kind of nonsense. (Looking at the history of the location, you see she calls for the same thing pretty much every weekend for the last year). I can pretty much guarantee no charges will be pressed, and she'll be calling back again next weekend for the same thing. Her pattern, our problem, and the police are the babysitters.

It isn't that calls like this have turned me, or tainted my being, or my perspective on humanity, but they do frustrate me. Similar calls happen every night, or like I have explained it is generally the same people. EMS has what we call frequent flyers. The same people who call for an ambulance every night. Usually, they need a ride across the city because a friend or family member or booty call lives close to one of the major hospitals. The ambulance gets them to the emergency department. They hop off the rig and sign a medical refusal form and walk away. The police have frequent flyer callers as well. Tainted, no, but it is a shame and a blatant waste of resources. That is all I am saying. I hang on to empathy, sympathy, and compassion, though some days it is just by a thread. I imagine, should those characteristics, those emotions dry up, then it will be time to retire my headset for good, regardless of how close or how far I am from a retirement date.

―――

Then there are the string of calls that just tend to annoy me. They get under my skin. The twenty-eight-year-old with an earache. The forty-one-year-old sprained an ankle. The four-year-old is refusing to go to bed. The ten-year-old is refusing to go to school. The grown woman whose friends left her at a party, and now she needs a ride home.

If you stub your toe so badly you decide to call 911, fine. When you are asked if your breathing is normal for you, think about it before you answer. If you are breathing like this *who-who-he-who-who-he-he-who-he-he-who* because your toe hurts? That is different from someone who has actual trouble breathing. You need an EMT (if you need an ambulance at all) and not a paramedic. You need a BLS rig, not an ALS rig. If you say trouble breathing because of the stubbed toe, a limited and variable resource is what we send. An ALS rig tied up for the stubbed toe could cause a serious delay in medical treatment for the person who calls next with trouble breathing, or for cardiac arrest.

During snowstorms and below freezing temperature winter periods, we get calls reporting icy roads. Okay, so slow down until a salt truck comes around? Buy better winter tires? What is it you possibly think 911 can do to help you when it comes to icy roads?

Calls in the spring, during a heavy rain, reporting water in the roads. I sometimes just want to tell the callers we will send the fire department out with mops and road squeegees. Do the fire departments have road squeegees? Ah, no. No, they most certainly do not.

I took a call once for the neighbor was snow-blowing his driveway at six thirty in the morning. This was an actual call. A racist call if you want to know the truth. Guy tells me, "My neighbor is outside snow blowing his driveway. It is six-thirty in the morning."

Naturally, I am struggling to see any emergency. And I say so.

"It's six-thirty in the morning."

"We had a lot of snow last night, maybe he has to get to work?"

"He won't have to get to work. He's a black guy," the caller said.

"Excuse me?" I asked.

"Yeah. The guy doesn't work."

"Perhaps a doctor appointment, or grocery shopping."

"At six-thirty in the morning? Nah, no. He's doing it to piss me off."

I was not planning on putting in a job. This call

went beyond ridiculous, but then the caller made matters worse.

"Better send the police to tell him to knock off the racket or I am gonna go over there and have words with him. He just moved onto the street this fall. I knew we were gonna have trouble with him."

I wanted to taunt the caller with, *Why is that, sir, because your new neighbor is black?* I just didn't think it was worth my time. And I doubted the caller was smart enough to pick up on the sarcasm.

Calls like that drive me nuts. They get right under my skin. I mentally chew on them over and over. I realize that since I started at ECD my overall love for people has fragmented. It happened a little at a time. I didn't think I could ever repair some of the loathing and disgust that has hardened around my heart.

At least two people are shot every night, more if you add up the shootings from each platoon. The same goes for the number of stabbings. I've lost count of how many overdoses come in a night. Ten? Twelve? That is just on First Platoon. Half make it. Half don't. So it goes.

# THE LANGUAGE LINE

One night I took a call from a man who asked for a Spanish interpreter. We use a company called Voiance for certified foreign language translators. It is a touch screen box, which we call a Vadon (auto-dial), on the phone screen monitor.

"Okay. Don't hang up," I told him. "You are going to hear a dial tone, but don't hang up." I had no idea if he understood anything I just said.

I reached up and pressed a Vadon on my screen. Only, I inadvertently hit the box next to Voiance, and instead clicked the one labeled LVAD. The LVAD Vadon rings into a hospital, specifically for left ventricular assist devices.

The doctor on the LVAD answered. I knew what I'd done. I'd created a party line between the doctor, the caller, and myself. This was not what I wanted.

As soon as the caller heard the doctor say hello, he began speaking in a panic but in Spanish.

"Sir, please hold on," I said, addressing the caller. "Doctor, this is nine-one-one. I inadvertently called the wrong service for assistance."

"That man sounds as if he is in distress," the doctor commented.

"Yes, sir. You can hang up," I instructed.

The Spanish-speaking person said, "I can hang up?" He spoke in broken English.

"No, sir. Not you. You don't hang up," I said to the caller.

"We might have someone here that speaks Spanish," the doctor said.

"No. No, that's okay. I called you by accident. You can disconnect the call," I said.

"Okay," the Spanish-speaking caller said. "Hang up now. You come?"

"No, sir," I said. "You cannot hang up."

The doctor said, "Hold on. Let me grab one of the nurses who speaks Spanish."

"Spanish. Yes, Spanish," my caller said.

"Doctor, that is not necessary."

He had put me on hold. Music now played in the background.

I didn't have time for this. I hit the Voiance Vadon.

"Sir, do not hang up," I continually instructed my caller. He must have understood a little English.

The Voiance interpreter answered. "What language, please?"

"Spanish," I said.

"Spanish, yes. Spanish!" the caller cried out.

Voiance connected me with a Spanish interpreter who gave me her employee ID number and told me to go ahead.

The caller began ranting. I didn't understand a word he said.

"Sir," I tried cutting in. "Sir, *un momento, por*

*favor.*" One Moment, please. The only Spanish I knew.

The doctor came back onto the line. "I can't find the nurse. She speaks Spanish."

"That's okay, doctor, you can hang up, please."

"I'm sorry," my interpreter interjected. "You want me to hang up?"

"No, ma'am. I need you to ask the caller what is the address of his emergency."

She translated my question to the caller. And, I guess, to the doctor.

"Wait," the doctor said. "Who is that?"

"I have a Spanish interpreter on the line, doctor. Please disconnect for me."

The caller was talking, as well, trying to give the interpreter his address.

"Does this man have a medical emergency?" Why was the doctor not just hanging up?

"I am trying to find out, sir. Can you please disconnect?"

"Okay," the doctor said. "Can I get information on where you are calling from?"

"Doctor, if you are going to insist on staying on this call I need you to STOP TALKING!"

I yelled at him. Loudly.

I looked around the room. Everyone watched me on this crazy call. My point was made, and the doctor stopped talking.

The translator gave me the address, and when I asked her to ask him to tell her "exactly what happened," my worst fears came true.

"He said, his house is on fire."

And it was. When the fire department arrived, the garage was fully engulfed in flames. The saving grace was that the garage was not attached to the house. He lost the structure, but no one was injured.

The entire call with all of the parties lasted just under ten minutes, about seven and a half minutes too long. Yes, there was some added confusion with the LVAD doctor on the line, but, unfortunately, calls requiring the language line services double job entry time. Translation, especially during medical calls, requires the back and forth of a lot of information. We go as fast as we can to enter jobs so responders can get dispatched, but we also have an obligation to make sure the information we get, and what we enter, is accurate.

# MENTAL HEALTH ARREST

FINDING BALANCE

# WHAT IS THE WORST CALL

I debated long and hard about the kind of calls I wanted to be included in this story. I could have filled the pages with horrific tales, or with the kinds of calls you have already read through. It seems like ten calls out of every eleven I take is *not* an actual emergency. Not to say the other ten calls aren't important, I am sure they are. We will make sure to send someone as soon as possible, they just aren't serious life and death emergencies, like *that* eleventh call.

I didn't want the book to be depressing. I just wanted to give a sliver sampling so you could taste some of the delectable gourmet offerings ladled onto our plates nightly.

When people I work with heard I was writing this book they asked if I was going to include this story or that story, or would say: "Remember that one time (at band camp)?"

This book has been over thirteen years in the making, and once I started writing, it went in, yet, different directions than I anticipated. It became important for sharing what I shared, if only for reasons important to me.

Any time I meet someone new I am always asked the same two questions. What is the craziest call you've ever received, and what is the worst call you've ever received? I have no problem sharing the crazy calls. They make for good storytelling, especially if everyone has had a few if you know what I mean.

The worst calls, I don't care to talk about. In fact, I have rarely, if ever, talked openly about the bad calls. They aren't something I want to relive. They aren't something I want to remember.

They are calls I will never forget. They do keep me awake at night. Or, if I am lucky enough to fall asleep, the worst calls wake me up. Countless nightmares and waking up in a cold sweat are common for me.

When I dream of the calls, they play out like horror movies in my head. Instead of just being on the other side of the phone, like I was in real life, I will find myself a floating observer. I am forced to watch the graphic incidents unfold from above.

It is those kinds of calls when we get home from work, we don't want to talk about our day, and may just want to be alone. Mow the lawn, as I indicated at the very beginning of the book. Talking about it may help some. For most of us, we just need the time to work it out in our own time, in our own way.

We have access to the Employee Assistance Program (EAP), which is a free service offering a wide variety of assistance to employees. Pretty evident from the name, I suppose. But this includes counseling. All kinds of counseling. And I know many people take full advantage of the services. It is always comforting when you know outside, professional help is available if, and when you need it.

It was during one night, in the middle of summer, when I took one of my worst calls ever. It wasn't a terribly busy night. I actually got some reading done. I had been making my way through C.J. Box's Joe Pickett series. Tearing through book after book. I remember I had the book I was currently reading, plus the next in the series in my bag, ready to go.

A call came in at about 0300, on this early July morning. I went through my Good Burger routine and the man on the other end of the line composed himself well enough to answer the questions asked.

I could see his location on the CAD map clearly enough based on his phone GPS. Good phones made finding people easier. Although never exact, and we needed to rely on where a caller stated the *where* of their emergency, GPS was definitely a helpful tool. He confirmed what the mapping terminal showed was a match.

The man was crying. No. Crying was not accurate. My caller was sobbing, hard. He kept sucking in air as if he struggled to breathe.

"Sir," I tried. "Can you tell me exactly what has happened?"

"My car. We went off the road," he said. "She's gone. She's gone."

It made my chest tighten. "Who's gone, sir?"

"She's gone."

"How many cars were involved in the accident," I asked.

"Just me. Just mine," he managed. He never stopped crying. Not once during the entire call.

"Okay, who's gone?"

"She is. She's gone."

I had a knot in the pit of my gut. I didn't get a flood of serious calls. Something like this immediately made me feel uneasy. "Where is she, sir?"

"Still in the car. She must have hit the windshield. Her head must have hit the windshield." He broke down. He cried out loud. He didn't hold anything back. "I can't believe this. I can't help her."

"Is she breathing?" I asked. I had the job entered in CAD. Police, the fire department, and an ambulance had been dispatched. With New CAD, I could find the responding units on the same mapping terminal where my caller was located.

Tiny fire truck, police car, and ambulance images moved like Pac-Man along the lines on the map, indicating streets. I could gauge their progress and get an idea of how far away they were from the accident scene.

They were far.

The man was in a very rural area, not close to the town he was in.

"She's not. She's not breathing. I'm telling you; she's gone."

"Okay," I said. Moving an injured person with head trauma could be dangerous. This woman wasn't breathing. It didn't get any more dangerous than that. "Let's get her out of the car."

"Move her?"

"Yes. We're going to get her out of the car, and onto the ground. Are you listening?"

"I'm trying."

"Is her seatbelt fastened?" I asked.

"It's not on. I don't know if she had one on. She hit the windshield. Her head hit the windshield."

I was worried my caller was going into shock. I wanted to keep him busy. I needed him to focus on his friend. "Take her out of the car, sir. Okay? Take her out of the car and lay her on the ground, not on any debris from the accident. Do you understand?"

I heard him grunting and struggling. I knew this couldn't be easy for him. I didn't want to imagine how badly banged up the woman was. I figured if her head hit the windshield and she wasn't breathing.

"I got her. I have her on the ground."

His crying became muffled. I pictured him laying over her body, the phone between them.

"Sir? Sir?" I tried getting his attention.

"She's gone. She is. She's gone."

I hated hearing him say this. He just kept repeating it. It would fill my nightmares, I knew. It would wake me whenever sleep took over. I did not want to hear his sobs anymore. I knew I didn't want to get stuck hearing them for the rest of my life.

"We're going to do CPR, okay?" I kept at him. "Sir? We're going to start compressions. Can you hear me?"

"I can hear you," he said. "What do I do?"

I told him to put his hand on her forehead and tilt her head back. Then I asked him to place his ear down near her mouth and asked if he could hear her breathing.

He couldn't.

I informed him, when we were ready, to place the heel of one hand on her chest, between her nipples, and the other onto the top of the first hand. I explained how we would do these compressions together, counting them off together.

"When I say now, you just put the phone down

but don't end the call, and we're going to count together, okay? Sir, okay?"

"Okay." He didn't sound convinced my plan would work, but for the moment he wasn't sobbing.

I kept looking at the mapping terminal. The responding units were getting very close to the location.

"Okay, sir. Now."

We counted compressions. "One. Two. Three..."

At some point, around sixty compressions in, the sound of his counting fell away. He was crying again.

"Sir?" I said.

"She's just gone. She's gone."

She was gone. I tried not to mourn with the caller. If I mourned every time I took a call like this, I would be in therapy for the rest of my life.

It still sinks in, though. I wanted us to be able to save her. I didn't want us to stop trying. I hoped for that miraculous recovery he was so confident would never happen. And when he was the one who was right, that she was gone, all I could do was tell him how sorry I was for his loss.

God, it sounded so empty. Hollow. It sounded how I felt.

And yet, I still said it a second time. "I'm so sorry for your loss."

I know he was draped over her body. I pictured him as clear as I could picture the smashed front end of his car, and the shattered, blood-soaked windshield.

He never answered me, but I heard the approaching sound of sirens closing in. I kept an eye on the job after the call disconnected. She had in fact expired on scene. She was only twenty-four years old. There was no indication the driver, my caller, had been drinking.

And I was right. His cries leak into nearly every dream I have.

However, a second after responders arrived on scene, and the call ended, I had no time to dwell on any of it.

The phone line rang. I had some other emergency waiting for me on the other end. All I can do is just keep going. One call after another. As much as I hoped my shift would have just ended, I still had hours to go. So I answer by the third ring, suck in a deep breath...

"This is nine-one-one. What is the address of your emergency?"

# DO THE RIGHT THING

I WAS ON PHONES TAKING EMERGENCY CALLS while working overtime on Third Platoon. It was midsummer and a typical nice warm Saturday night.

The calls came in one after the other. The variety of calls was all over the place, too. Dirt bikes raced up and down city streets wreaking havoc. Unlicensed and usually without helmets, the bikers were a menace to automobile drivers. People shot off fireworks, generating calls from neighbors annoyed with the never-ending whistle-boom making it impossible for residents to sleep.

I took the next call. "This is nine-one-one. What is the address of your emergency?"

"They're hurting my dad." A child caller. They were crying, and hard to understand. I managed to extract an address. It was for an apartment complex in Spencerport.

"Where are you?" I asked the young girl on the other end of the line.

"I'm hiding in the bathroom. My dad told me to stay in the bathroom and not come out. But they're hurting him."

"Are the people who are hurting him inside your house?"

"No. They're outside. In the back area where the picnic tables are," she said. I could hear a verbal confrontation.

"Is that your dad I hear? Is he yelling at someone?"

"Yes. That's him."

"How many people are out back with your dad?" I put in a job for the police to respond. FGHTA. It was the best event type for the moment until I could get a better idea of what was taking place. I felt a tightening in my own chest. Things sounded as if they were escalating. The fear in my caller's voice resonated in my ears.

"There are four people out there with him."

"Were you out there with him when this started?" I asked.

"Yes," she said. She still cried but did great answering my questions.

"Did you see any weapons?"

"One of them had a baseball bat," she told me.

I upgraded the event to a WEAPA. It changed the dynamics of the response. I couldn't imagine what this child was going through. I know the palms of my hands were sweating. I kept checking to see how far away the police were. "Okay," I said. "And what did you do?"

"My dad told me to get inside and lock myself in the bathroom."

It didn't sound good. I wondered if her father knew the people out back. "How old are you?"

"Nine."

"Nine? Well, you are doing a great job. You have

been able to answer all of my questions. Can you see your dad from the bathroom?"

"Kind of. Through the screen in the window," she said. "Are the police coming?"

"They are," I assured her. I hated that she could see outside. I wished she wouldn't look. I didn't want to tell her that, because her information was helpful, but neither did I want her to witness anyone swing a baseball bat at her father's head. "And I am going to stay on the phone with you until they get there. Okay?"

She said okay, but I could barely hear her. I heard her father yelling. I couldn't make out what he said. There were more raised voices. If they weren't actively fighting at the moment, it sounded as if things could go south at any second.

"What was happening out there tonight?" I asked.

"We were cooking hamburgers and hot dogs, and these kids came over and started swearing and smoking cigarettes, and my dad asked them to take it somewhere else," she explained.

"How old are these kids?"

"I don't know. They go to high school," she said.

A few seconds later a few police cars pulled up. They dispersed the group, as far as I could tell. "Hey," I told my young caller. "You did a really good job tonight. I am proud of how brave you were."

"Thank you." She didn't sound convinced.

Afterward, when the call was completed, I took down the information for the job and submitted the call to a committee for Rochester's Do The Right Thing Award. At the end of summer, I was notified that my child caller was one of only a few who would be honored at a ceremony downtown, and I was invited to share the experience. The Deputy mayor was also present, and a host of photographers. The kids receiving the awards were given backpacks filled with school supplies, as well as a trophy for their heroics.

---

People ask all the time how I can do a job like this. I am often told by others, they did not think they could ever do what I did.

I explain how calls like my worst call and doing the right thing are the reason why I come to work every day. I couldn't save that woman who died in the car accident, but I tried. I hope my efforts, and my staying calm provided comfort to the man who lost his friend. I will never know.

Keeping a child company while they hide, fearful the worst is about to happen to their family had me unnerved. I knew this child could either see out of the bathroom window or at the very least, hear everything taking place beyond the mesh screen. The young girl had been terrified, but I believe I kept her from losing control until police arrived on scene.

I know it is only two small examples in an entire book filled with calls, but at the end of the day, when I leave work, I often feel like I made an impact, a difference. Things don't always work out, don't always go well, but as long as I do my best to help while getting help to those in need, then I know I am making a dent against a disturbed society, demented and deranged humanity. If you think that sounds melodramatic, come and sit with me for a shift. Listen to calls. I think by the end of eight hours you will be in full agreement.

There is a feeling of accomplishment I receive when I know I've done all the things possible for the best outcome. This is how and this is why I can do the job I do. Pride may be sinful, but I am oftentimes filled with it, with pride as well as a sense of gratitude, and thankfulness. When I tell people I am a 911 Dispatcher, my chest might puff out some, and my head may stand a little higher on my shoulders.

# LIBATIONS (CHOIR PRACTICE) / RELATIONSHIPS

CHOIR PRACTICE IS WHAT WE CALL IT WHEN AT the end of a shift everyone is invited out to a bar for something to eat and some drinks. On First Platoon there are only two bars open at 0800 that I am aware of. One served bar food, one did not. You can guess which of the two we most regularly frequented.

Giant fried bologna sandwiches, burgers, waffle french fries, and beer. The jukebox is on, but the music isn't loud. This way we can talk without screaming to one another. Sometimes there are another one or two people in the bar, but we largely dominate a place at eight in the morning.

Throwing darts, shooting pool, and just talking about anything that isn't work-related.

The beers go down easy. A little too easily most mornings.

Choir Practice is synonymous with team building, and friendship bonding. Tends to have a lot of clap on the back, and knuckle punch in terms of endearment. Also, the chance to talk openly and freely about things that occur. Whatever *things* might be on that particular morning. Most nights the idea of morning choir practice sounds good, until morning rolls around, and I am tired. I mostly just want to go home. Friends convince me just to stop in, have one.

Which I do. I stop in. I have one, and then another. Usually four hours later, and I find myself belting out songs in competition with the jukebox.

I try not to let this happen too often. Once a week at the most. (I kid. I kid). It has happened far too many times, but not as often as one might think. Or remember. That eternal search for balance, I suppose.

I do spend my time outside of work mostly with friends from work. Not just at choir practice, though. Don't get me wrong. Libations are almost always involved. We go to breakfast, lunches, and dinners. We go kayaking, camping, and to the movies. We go to weddings, birthday parties, and retirement parties. Yes, we meet for drinks. We walk our dogs, we have bonfires, and we help each other move. We help each other with whatever help is needed, whenever it is needed.

We argue. We fight. We kiss and we make up. My work family is highly dysfunctional, but I wouldn't want them any other way. They get me. I get them. We are the few who get each other.

While at work we talk about sex, drugs, drinking, anal bleaching, and pooping at work vs pooping at home. We discuss current love interests, former lovers, and hopeful potentials. We talk about food, food, and food. We watch Spongebob Square Pants, Ridiculousness, and Catfish. We watch the Food Network, the Olympics, baseball, basketball, and football. And then we talk more about food.

There is an old saying. Don't shit where you eat. Pretty straightforward. I suppose it can be applied to many of life's lessons. In the case of ECD, I consider it to mean not getting involved with coworkers, or subordinates. Romantically, that is.

ECD is where I make my money. This job. Why risk a hostile work environment when things go bad? Because things always go bad. At least, for me, they do. It is something I have, personally, gotten used to.

We all know coworkers unconcerned by a fortune-cookie attitude. They are in every center, police and fire department, and ambulance base. They eat where they shit. A lot of 'em have shit they eat at home, too.

I am not speaking out of school. *So it goes*, if you know what I mean?

My guess is that kind of thing extends beyond the First Responder arena. It is what it is. I, personally, think it best not to get involved with people I work with. However, I am not having a lot of luck getting (seriously) involved with people who don't work at ECD, either.

It boils down to a simple fact. You do what you have to do, and I won't judge. Hopefully, if you see me doing what I have to do, it is the same judge-free zone. Is it that we are all searching for happiness, and think the only place to find it is while we are with someone else?

So, for this last section of the book, I want to take you, my new *bestie*, out of the workplace. I know we discussed a golf outing earlier, but this is a bit different now.

Here. Now. We are going to briefly explore my

constant plight for balance. Where I have achieved minor success, and areas where I still struggle, and maybe, together make a plan on how to do things differently, or at the very least, better?

Balance is something that often eludes me, and maybe I sabotage everything good, or good for me. Not on purpose, mind you. And yet the sabotaging occurs time and time again.

I've gotten quite used to being on my own, on being alone. It isn't terrible. Am I happy, though? This is the nagging question that fucks with my head and my heart. Am I happy, though?

My kids and my Ziti make me happy. I just wonder if that happiness is the same kind I need for a sustainable future into old age, and into my retirement (golden) years. I hate thinking like this, but Ziti won't be with me forever, and my kids have lives of their own.

What will I do if I end up alone, forever? Get another dog? Hope my kids visit more? Or at some point, will I meet the right person for me? I hope that happens, that I meet someone. The right one. Could she be out there? I am not going to hold my breath.

Is it possible I have reached a point where I no longer believe there is someone out there for me? A perfect match? Or have I come across plenty, and then just let them get away?

Or pushed them away?

Or, I myself, slinked away?

If I do wreck my relationships on purpose, it is a subconscious severing or mangling. Generally. If I am honest, sometimes I *am* aware. I know I am about to fuck things up. And then I do. With skilled follow-through, or great abandonment. I guess it depends on how you look at it.

What I realize, though, is that I am not *really* alone. It may be more of a curse of First Responders than some mental health issue I suffer from all alone.

I work with people who have messed-up relationships, just like me. Some may not realize it, but the truth is brilliantly obvious. To me, anyway. Those people have more than I have, but I sometimes think what they have is not something I would want, anyway.

Don't get me wrong, we even have several couples who met at ECD and are successfully married. (To each other). I applaud that, as well as wonder about the "science" behind it.

I may not want to shit where I eat, but perhaps, I need to find someone who also works in the First Responder ... let's call it *genre*. Meeting someone who gets the hours, the missed holidays, the not wanting to talk for extended periods of time? (But then I think back to the eating where I shit). Six of one, half a dozen of the other, right?

I do know I am not giving up on finding the right person, I just know my time to do so decreases day by day. Ziti and I have become pretty set in our ways. I am not opposed to meeting someone; I just wonder if that is in the cards for me. I keep an open mind, and an open heart, and Ziti and I will always accept applications for the perfect companion.

Pretty soon, I suppose, I will be yelling at neighbor kids to get off my lawn. It's not much to look forward to, but it is something. Isn't it?

Hell. Who knows? Maybe this book rocks the

memoir field and I am invited to guest speak at an array of venues across the country, the publisher beginning for a follow-up, and George R. R. Martin and I throw back shots of *Jameson* laughing about books we may or may never write in the future.

# FINDING THE BALANCE

In *12 Years a Cubicle Slave*, author Joshua Osenga said: "Balance is a feeling derived from being whole and complete; it's a sense of harmony. It is essential to maintaining quality in life and work."

Balance? Is it actually attainable? Is it sustainable?

I do have balance. I may wobble, and I may falter. I definitely falter, and stumble...

An example of stumbling, of faltering? I smoke. I quit smoking. Then I buy a pack of cigarettes. Then I quit. Before I know it, I am bumming a pack from my brother, sister, or mother. Then I quit again. Up. Down. Up ... Down. Up. Down. Updown ... Quit. Smoke. Quit. Smoke. Quitsmoke ... often, but it has been a long, long time since I have fallen down.

I still may fall down in the future, in fact, I am certain I will. I just think as long as I don't lose sight of where I get my balance, I shouldn't have much trouble picking myself up.

Other than what I have written here, I have no answers. I am not a philosopher. Most of the time I don't even take my own advice about anything. The simple truth is I live simplistically. One day at a time. It is really all we can do.

It is really all *I* can do.

I do like my beer. And I do enjoy the company of women. I don't think that is where I find my balance. I enjoy reading and read between eighty-five and one hundred books a year. My house is filled with full bookcases. There must be a thousand on display, and another thousand in airtight totes in my basement. I also write, obviously. Usually, I write fiction. I have twenty-nine small press published novels, and books in just about every genre. I have written horror novels, a fantasy book series, some science fiction, books for young adults, adventure, and even a contemporary romance novel, *Before the Sun Sets*. I do find balance when writing. When I am writing, I am able to put a bit of myself into each character I create.

There is something about the creative process that fulfills me. I find writing soothing, and the process relieves stress. Generally, like with this book, I write for an audience of one. Me. Naturally, I want others to read the books I've written. It's just not the reason I am writing them. I don't expect fame, or—God willing—fortune. Would those things be nice? A season series picked up by Netflix or Amazon Prime? You bet that would be nice. Awesome, in fact. Again, though, it is not why I write.

Surprisingly, writing this book has given me greater balance than any other I have ever written, and I know the reason why.

This book forced me to take an honest look at my life, the hurdles I've made it over, and the obstacles still set before me, and with a sense of calm, I am overwhelmed by the journey. I am, actually, happy about the road I find myself traveling down.

I expect the unexpected at every turn. Sometimes, because things are going so well, I figure the other shoe has got to drop at some point. What do I mean by that? How long can a person go on feeling good before something bad happens to them? That's what I mean.

It is as if I am just waiting for something awful to happen.

I see it day in and day out at 911. The *awful* happens 24/7 without taking a break. It has to catch up to me eventually. Do you ever feel that way? Like the other shoe has got to drop sooner or later?

Yeah. Me, too. And I hate feeling that way.

For what it is worth, I also play a little guitar. Not an actual small guitar. It is a regular-sized guitar. I just mean I am not very good at it. I play it now and again. The worst part is my singing. It is bad.

I was singing in my car once. Came up to a red light. I had my windows down. Why not? It had been a beautiful summer day. The car pulled up next to me. Old car. What I would call a beater. You know the kind where the A/C can't possibly work? Anyway, when they got next to me, they put their windows up. They choose stifling summer heat at a red light over listening to me belt out a Lou Gramm / Foreigner song. Like my writing, though, when I play guitar and sing it is for my enjoyment, no one else's. (And when I sing, trust me, no one else is enjoying it).

The last two things that help me decompress, that bring me balance, are spending time with my kids, and now grandkids, and spending time with Ziti.

First off, Ziti was a rescue dog. Some say I rescued

her. In truth, she rescued me. I never realized how empty my life—working, living alone—had become, until she entered my life. I think about her when I am at work. At the end of a long shift, all I want is to get home and play with her. Throw the ball around in the backyard or walk down the pier at Charlotte beach. She may not say it, (mainly because she can't talk), but I know she feels the same way.

All three of my kids have proven themselves resilient. They are full-grown adults. They all graduated from college. As I have stated, Phil works an opposite platoon and wheel than I do. And that just sucks. However, we do our best to see each other as often as possible. Grant graduated *Cum Laude* from Alfred University. He owns a house in the same town I live in and will be getting married this fall. I do get to see him and his fiancee more often. Raeleigh has her MBA in accounting from Niagara University. My daughter stayed in Buffalo well after graduation, which is only around sixty miles away but manages to come to town a few times every couple of months, or I head out her way for an evening of breweries, burgers, and darts. Getting together with the kids is always and will always be a highlight for me. Grant, who owns a pretty big house, will host bonfires, inviting everyone over. We eat, have some drinks, play some games, and really—really—visit.

The laughing we all do when we are together—nothing beats that. Nothing.

And the best part, for me, is hugging them hello. Phil and Stephanie, Grant and Abby, and Raeleigh and Anthony. I love giving and getting hugs from them. My boys are both taller than me. I have no problem putting my head on their chest and giving them a squeeze, and they don't seem to mind. My daughter is a bit more fragile. I wrap an arm around her and try not to crush her as I kiss the top of her head.

I know at the end of each shift, long after I am home and laying in bed awake and unable to sleep, I did my best. I followed policies the best I could and got help from those in need. Sometimes things worked out for the callers. Sometimes things did not work out. Most of the time, I never get any closure. I have no idea what happened to them, any of them. I have balance from knowing I did all I could. I take each and every call seriously, even though many are ridiculous and not 911-worthy. I gather information, start help based on the information, and do all I could to keep responders safe. There is balance in doing the job. I have found balance there. It took me a while to realize it. Balance does exist in the work I do, have done, and will continue doing for several more years.

Between these wonderful things, and Libations (Choir Practice), I would say yes, I have found a pretty solid sense of balance. For that, I am thankful.

And then, there are other parts of my life where the balance is lacking and will be an aspect I strive to improve. Fingers crossed.

# LOOKING TOWARD RETIREMENT

I DID HAVE THE AMAZING OPPORTUNITY OF taking my middle son and daughter, and their significant others, on a trip a few years back. We spent a week in Alaska. A week is not nearly enough time to explore such a giant state. We stayed in Anchorage, but journeys to Seward, and up to Fairbanks, stopping to see Mt. Denali on the way. We climbed glaciers, hiked mountains, took a dip in a natural hot spring, and boat-*ed* out to the Gulf of Alaska.

That was the first vacation I had taken in over fourteen years. I had time off from work before, naturally, but never went anywhere. Couldn't afford to really go anywhere with my kids. Sure, I could have gone places on my own. It would have been cheaper, but I didn't want to. If I couldn't go with them, I didn't want to go anywhere. So I saved and saved. When I could cover the cost of most of the trip, we booked the week on the opposite end of the country. An absolutely beautiful state.

I plan on traveling in *my* future. All the time. I want to see all of the United States. And Europe.

And Australia ... Do you get the idea? I have some making-up on lost time to rectify.

The kids are talking about seeing Italy for our next big trip, *eh-oh, oh-eh!*

In the meantime, I am doing all I can, to save as much as possible, so that in a few years I can hang up my headset and move north. I am one of the few who does not plan to move south when I retire. I don't mind winters (and if I have no place to be because I am retired, I won't mind them all the more).

I am ready to be done. That is the short truth of it all. I am tired. I am ready to be done. Socking away extra here and there could be the difference between leaving in seven years or being forced to work another ten.

I do not want to be here for another ten years. I don't think I can do that. Not mentally.

# AFTERWARD

There is no *real* end to this book, other than right here. 911 calls will continue coming in, and as long as I am employed with the ECD, I will continue collecting stories.

I said at the beginning the book is really about me and finding my balance. That is also not a definite thing. It is a work in progress. It is something I admittedly struggle with on a regular, if not daily, basis.

Part of me knows I will continue this saga with stories gathered from 911 workers from across the country. That might be a book to keep an eye out for, as well.

If you made it this far, I can't thank you enough for your time and attention. My disjointed, nonlinear way of telling a story was done on purpose. It is meant to keep you off-balance while reading. I wanted it to provide an atmosphere of literary chaos. I hope more than anything you enjoyed the memoirs I put forth and are able to take something away from the tales told. While all are absolutely true, enough of the small details were changed to ensure no one's privacy

# AFTERWARD

was invaded. That doesn't change the point, impact, or sincerity at all.

As I dream of one day hanging up my headset for good, my hearing ruined from the constant soft static in one ear, I know I will always look back on my career and think Holy Shit. I was a part of that?

Aside from workplace politics and antiquated antics, aside from outside and inside department head egos, and overall childish behavior by all, I enjoy what I do. I take gratification in my work day in and day out. When I tell someone I am a 911 Dispatcher, I know I always say it full of pride.

Pride might be considered sinful, but I can't hide the way my career has made me feel. I also take comfort in the brotherhood and sisterhood of the families represented on the colorful First Responder Flag.

The Red is for Firefighters. The Blue for Law Enforcement. The White is for EMS and Doctors. The Green is for the Military. Our Military. The Grey is for Corrections Officers. The White with a Red Stripe through the center is for Nurses. And last, but definitely, not least is the Gold Stripe for Dispatchers and TCCs.

If so inclined, download a scanner app. Listen to us in your home, and your car. We are the voice on the other side of the radio. We are First When Seconds Count ... I have heard this said and it sticks with me, although I am not aware of who said it: " 911 Dispatchers are some of the most important people you will *never* see!"

PT3
October 2022

# SPECIAL THANKS

In alphabetical order, I want to call out my Beta Readers for the wonderful, and insightful job they did with reading through many, many drafts of this book. They also provided invaluable feedback. Without them, this story wouldn't be half as good as I believe it is:

Tammie Baker, Earl Cutlip, Joy Carr, Steve Cusenz, D. Jeremy DeMar, Travis Dobrowski, Morgan Gleisle, Katie Kast (K-Pop), Marcus Kratts, Rachel A. Kohl, Patrick Maar, Christopher Martin, Lisa Rice, Shelli Rodenbaug Shear, Craig Spade, Joshua Taylor, and Charles Vitale.

# GLOSSARY OF TERMS

**ALJ** - Administrative Law Judge is an executive judge for official and unofficial administrative disputes in the federal government.

**ALS** - Advanced Life Support ambulance - Has an EMT- Paramedic on board, and is equipped with airway support equipment, cardiac life support, cardiac monitors, and carries and can administer medications.

**BLS** - Basic Life Support ambulance - provides transportation when medically necessary. Has an EMT on board and care can include the administration of oxygen and other non-invasive procedures.

**CAD** - Computer-Aided Dispatching - systems utilized by dispatchers and call takers to prioritize and record incident calls, identify the status and location of responders in the field, and effectively dispatch responder personnel.

## GLOSSARY OF TERMS

**CAD Mask** - are dedicated lines used for entering an address, the caller's name, phone number, and the details of the emergency.

**DISPATCHER I** - A person who can dispatch either Police cars or Fire / EMS

**DISPATCHER II** - A Dispatcher II is a promotional position. If someone is a Dispatcher I, either as a Police Dispatcher or a Fire Dispatcher, once promoted they learn how to dispatch on the opposite side of the room. Once certified they can Dispatch Police / Fire / EMS, as well as work as a TCC.

**ECD** - The Emergency Communications Department of the City of Rochester operating the Monroe County 911 Center.

**EEOC** - The U.S. Equal Employment Opportunity Commission is a federal agency that was established via the Civil Rights Act of 1964 to administer and enforce civil rights laws against workplace discrimination.

**EMT** - Emergency Medical Technician - An EMT can give emergency care to people outside or on the way to the hospital giving basic medical and first-aid care to a patient.

**MAN WORKING** - I work this day for you. You work this day for me. The two working dates must be within thirty days of one another. And, dammit, not an hour beyond that thirty-day limit!

## GLOSSARY OF TERMS

**NYSDHR** - New York State Division of Human Rights is a New York State agency created to enforce the state's Human Rights Law. The Division is a unit of the New York State Executive Department.

**ORDER** - When below Staffing Minimums, someone is forced to work an additional one to eight hours after the completion of their scheduled shift.

**PARAMEDIC** - Can provide life-saving treatment, including the administration of medication, starting an IV, and providing advanced airway management.

**PAR** - Personnel Accountability Report of every person at the scene of a fire, or any other dangerous/hazardous type of incident

**PLATOON** - There are three (3) platoons (and three (3) wheels) - coupled together giving 24/7 coverage at ECD
    First Platoon - Midnight to 8 AM (0000-0800)
    Second Platoon - 8 AM to 4 PM (0800-1600)
    Third Platoon - 4 PM to Midnight (1600-0000)

**POD** - A section or group of positions in the same area. (Fire Pod, Police Pod, Supervisor Pod, Several TCC Pods)

**RFD** - Rochester Fire Department

**RPD** - Rochester Police Department

**TCC** - A 911 Operator who takes the emergency phone calls

## GLOSSARY OF TERMS

**VACATION PICKS** - Guaranteed one to four weeks time off. The weeks are selected at the beginning of the year. Any other time off is not guaranteed. (This pick list is done by seniority). Could be a few years before you get a week off in the summer, or during holidays like Christmas and Thanksgiving.

**VOIANCE** - Certified foreign language interpreters

**WHEEL** - There are three (3) wheels (and three (3) platoons) - coupled together giving 24/7 coverage at ECD

# SAMPLE PLATOON CALENDAR

| Monday | Tuesday | Wednesday | Thursday | Friday | Saturday | Sunday |
|--------|---------|-----------|----------|--------|----------|--------|
| 1 | 2 | 3 | 4 | 5 OFF | 6 OFF | 7 |
| 8 | 9 | 10 | 11 OFF | 12 OFF | 13 | 14 |
| 15 | 16 | 17 OFF | 18 OFF | 19 | 20 | 21 |
| 22 | 23 OFF | 24 OFF | 25 | 26 | 27 | 28 |
| 29 OFF | 30 OFF | 31 | | | | |

Days Off in shaded Blue, Working Days in non-shaded White

# CURRENT MONROE COUNTY FIRE DEPARTMENTS

**East Side**
Bushnell's Basin
Brighton
Egypt
East Rochester
Fairport
Henrietta
Honeoye Falls
Irondequoit
Mendon
Penfield
Pittsford
Point Pleasant
Rush
Sea Breeze
St. Paul
Webster
West Webster

**West Side**
Barnard
Brockport
Chili
Churchville
Clifton
Gates
Hamlin / Morton / Walker
Hilton
Lakeshore
Mumford
North Greece
Ridge Road
Scottsville
Spencerport
Rochester Fire Department (both east/west)

# CURRENT MONROE COUNTY AMBULANCE CORPS

American Medical Response
Brighton
Chili / Henrietta / Scottsville
Hamlin
Irondequoit
Penfield
Pittsford
Webster

Monroe Ambulance
Brockport
Gates
Honeoye Falls
North East Quadrant
Perinton
Rochester Institute of Technology

# CURRENT MONROE COUNTY POLICE DEPARTMENTS

Rochester Police Department
Irondequoit
Webster
Greece
Ogden
East Rochester
N.Y.S. Troopers
City Security
City/County Parks

Monroe County Sheriff's Office
Brighton
Gates
Brockport
Fairport
Fairport
Animal Control
City Parking

## ABOUT THE AUTHOR

**Phillip Tomasso** is the Amazon Bestselling author of twenty-nine previous novels, including *Sounds of Silence, Before the Sun Sets, You Choose,* and *Temple of Shadow. Nothing Good Happens After Midnight* is his first work of nonfiction. Working full-time as a Fire/EMS Dispatcher at 911, he lives in Rochester, NY with his pitbull rescue, Ziti.

---

To learn more about Phillip Tomasso and discover more Next Chapter authors, visit our website at www.nextchapter.pub.

Nothing Good Happens After Midnight
ISBN: 978-4-82415-534-4
Mass Market

Published by
Next Chapter
2-5-6 SANNO
SANNO BRIDGE
143-0023 Ota-Ku, Tokyo
+818035793528

21st December 2022

www.ingramcontent.com/pod-product-compliance
Lightning Source LLC
LaVergne TN
LVHW032008070526
838202LV00059B/6354